edges

Assessment for Learning in English

Lindsay McNab

Imelda Pilgrim

Marian Slee

Series consultant: Susan Sutton

1

www.heinemann.co.uk

✓ Free online support
✓ Useful weblinks
✓ 24 hour online ordering

01865 888058

Heinemann is an imprint of Pearson Education Limited, a company incorporated in England and Wales, having its registered office at Edinburgh Gate, Harlow, Essex, CM20 2JE.
Registered company number: 872828

Heinemann is a registered trademark of Pearson Education Limited

© Pearson Education Limited, 2004

First published 2004

09 08
10 9 8 7 6

British Library Cataloguing in Publication Data is available from the British Library on request.

ISBN 978 0 435227 20 3

Cover design by Wooden Ark Studio   Designed by Wooden Ark Studio   Printed and bound in China (GCC/06)
Cover photo: © Alamy   Produced by Kamae Design

Original illustrations © Harcourt Education Limited, 2004

Illustrated by **Johanna Barco:** pp37, 72, 77, 103, 110; **Abigail Conway:** pp7, 25, 26; **Andy Elkerton:** pp15, 17, 140; **Phil Healey:** pp43, 75, 117; **Paul McCaffery:** pp10, 33; **Andrew Morris:** pp65, 143, 148, 151, 154, 156, 159, 164, 168, 174; **Sarah Warburton:** pp70, 90, 139; **Jennifer Ward:** p61.

Photos: p20 Getty Images UK/Hulton Archive; pp38, 59, 67 Getty Images UK/PhotoDisc; p39 Kobal Collection/Original Films/Bob Marshak; p40 Ronald Grant Archive/Original Films; pp44, 58, 71, 74, 114 Corbis; pp54, 55 Microsoft Corporation; pp63, 64 Science Photo Library; p79 Harcourt Education Ltd/Jim Chanel; pp82, 105, 108 Alamy; p86 Rex Features; p100 ANT Photo Library/Michael Cermak; pp101, 104 Kobal Collection/Discovery Channel/MGM/Greg Barrett; p123(T) Getty Images UK/Digital Vision; p123(B) Digital Vision; pp131, 132 NHPA; p139 Eidos Interactive; p140(T) Kobal Collection/United Artists/Danjaq/EA; p140(M) Ronald Grant Archive/New Line Cinema/Warner Brothers.

Acknowledgements
Every effort has been made to contact copyright holders of material reproduced in this book. Any omissions will be rectified in subsequent printings if notice is given to the publishers.

'The Ghost at Ivy Cottage' from *Short and Scary: A Book of Very Short Scary Stories* by Louise Cooper, published by OUP 2002. Reprinted with permission of Oxford University Press; 'Faces' from *The Shirt From A Hanged Man's Back* by Dennis Hamley, published by Andre Deutsch. Copyright © Dennis Hamley. Reprinted with the kind permission of the author; 'A Night at a Cottage' from *A Moment of Time* by Richard Hughes. Copyright © Richard Hughes. Reprinted with permission of David Higham Associates Limited; 'For Word' and 'Poetics' from *Funky Chickens* by Benjamin Zephaniah, published by Viking 1996. Copyright © Benjamin Zephaniah 1996. Reprinted with permission of The Penguin Group UK; Review of '2 Fast 2 Furious' from the *Funday Times*, No 737, October 26th 2003. Copyright © Times Newspapers Limited 2003. Reprinted with permission; Blue Planet leaflet. Reprinted with permission of Blue Planet Aquarium; Adverts from the 'Beat Poverty Campaign', Save the Children. Reprinted with the kind permission of Save the Children; 'Branded a Fool' poster. Copyright © Crown Copyright August 2002, Department of Trade and Industry. Reprinted with permission; 'Poem for a Dead Poet' by Roger McGough, from *The Works* edited by Paul Cookson, published by Macmillan. Copyright © 2000 by Roger McGough. Reprinted by permission of PFD on behalf of Roger McGough; 'Reader: But What is Poetry?' by Adrian Mitchell, from *The Orchard Book of Poems*, published by Orchard Books. Copyright © Adrian Mitchell 1993. Reprinted by permission of PFD on behalf of Adrian Mitchell. *Educational Health Warning! Adrian Mitchell asks that none of his poems are used in connection with any examinations whatsoever!*; extract from 'Poetry' by Eleanor Farjeon, from *Blackbird Has Spoken* published by Macmillan. Reprinted by permission of David Higham Associates Limited; 'Spell' from *The Good Child's Guide to Rock 'n' Roll* by Carol Ann Duffy, published by Faber and Faber Limited. Copyright © Carol Ann Duffy. Reprinted by permission of Faber and Faber Limited; extract from 'The Warm and the Cold' from *Season Songs* by Ted Hughes, published by Faber and Faber Limited. Copyright © Ted Hughes. Reprinted with permission of Faber and Faber Limited; extract from 'At the End of a School Day' by Wes Magee, from *The Works* edited by Paul Cookson, published by Macmillan. Copyright © Wes Magee. Reprinted with the kind permission of the author; extract from 'Be a Butterfly' by Grace Nichols from *The Fat Black Woman's Poems* published by Virago. Copyright © Grace Nichols 1984. Reproduced with permission of Curtis Brown Ltd, London, on behalf of Grace Nichols; extract from 'Praise of a Collie' by Norman MacCaig, from *Collected Poems* by Norman MacCaig, published by Chatto & Windus. Used by permission of The Random House Group Limited; extract from 'The Highwayman' by Alfred Noyes. Reprinted by permission of The Society of Authors as the Literary Representative of the Estate of Alfred Noyes; extract from 'Reggae Sounds' by Linton Kwesi Johnson. Copyright © Linton Kwesi Johnson. Reproduced by kind permission of LKJ Music Publishers Limited; extract from 'The Lake Isle of Innisfree' by W B Yeats. Reprinted by permission of A P Watt Limited on behalf of Michael B Yeats; extract from 'Wurd Up' by Martin Glynn, from *The Works* edited by Paul Cookson, published by Macmillan. Copyright © Martin Glynn. Reprinted with the kind permission of the author; 'Talking Turkeys' by Benjamin Zephaniah, from *Talking Turkeys* by Benjamin Zephaniah, published by Viking 1994. Copyright © Benjamin Zephaniah 1994. Reprinted with permission of The Penguin Group UK; 'Dragonflies' by Joan Poulson, from *The Works 2* edited by Paul Cookson, published by Macmillan. Copyright © Joan Poulson. Reprinted with the kind permission of the author; extracts from *Chinese Cinderella* by Adeline Yen Mah, published by Penguin 1999. Copyright © Adeline Yen Mah, 1999. Reprinted by permission of The Penguin Group UK; extracts of text and illustrations from *Ethel & Ernest* by Raymond Briggs, published by Jonathan Cape. Used by permission of The Random House Group Limited; extracts from *The Crocodile Hunter* by Steve & Terri Irwin. Reprinted by permission of The Orion Publishing Group Limited; extracts from ChildLine website. Reprinted with the kind permission of ChildLine www.childline.org.uk; 'Smoking Sucks' from *Mizz*, No 488, January 28th – February 10th 2004. Copyright © Mizz/IPC Syndication. Used with permission of IPC Syndication; extracts from Battersea Dogs Home website. www.dogshome.org. Reprinted with the kind permission of Battersea Dogs Home; extract from *The Time Machine* by H G Wells. Reprinted with permission of A P Watt Limited on behalf of the Literary Executors of the Estate of H G Wells; extract from the 'Prologue' from *The Lord of the Rings* by J. R. R. Tolkien, published by HarperCollins Publishers. Reprinted with permission of the publishers; extract from the film *Goldfinger*. Copyright © 1964 Danjaq Inc and United Artists Corporation. All rights reserved. Reprinted with the kind permission Eon/Danjaq, LLC; extracts from *Artemis Fowl* by Eoin Colfer published by Viking 2001. Copyright © Eoin Colfer 2001. Reprinted with permission of Penguin Group UK; extracts from *Artemis Fowl: The Arctic Incident* by Eoin Colfer, published by Puffin 2002. Copyright © Eoin Colfer 2002. Reprinted with permission of the Penguin Group UK.

Contents

The following icons are used in this book:

 This indicates that **next steps** activities and teaching notes are available in the Assessment and Resource File 1 and Teacher's Handbook 1

 This indicates that a supplementary activity, or worksheet to support a Student Book activity, is available in the Assessment and Resource File 1

Introduction

The whole picture

In this book you will explore how writers write, readers read, speakers speak and listeners listen. You will develop skills in assessing your own learning and working out what you need to do to make good progress. By the end of the book we hope you will feel in control and ready to move on.

WHAT? You will:
- become a sharper and more perceptive reader
- develop your talents as a writer
- gain confidence and skill as a speaker and a listener
- take control of your own learning

HOW? by:
- reading a range of lively, interesting and focused texts
- experimenting with different writing styles and techniques
- working with other students in formal and informal situations
- assessing your work and using the feedback and progress checks to track your learning and set your own targets

WHY? because:
- better reading skills help you understand and interpret your world
- writing is an important form of communication
- increasing your confidence in speaking and listening helps you deal effectively with different situations
- when you know what you are learning, and why you are learning it, you make better progress

1 Dreadful tales

The bigger picture

In this unit you will explore how writers structure stories and develop character and setting. At the end of the unit you will plan, draft and revise a short story of your own.

WHAT? **You will:**
- identify how some writers start, develop and end short stories
- learn how to show character through description, dialogue and action
- discover how to involve the reader by using narrative devices

HOW? **by:**
- examining the structure of three short stories
- thinking about how description, dialogue and action are used to create character
- exploring writers' methods and developing these in your own writing

WHY? **because:**
- it will help you to understand more about the craft of writing
- you need to be able to comment on and explain writers' choices
- to be a good writer you need to plan ahead and check back

Structure of a story

Stories can often be broken down into five stages. The notes alongside the story below highlight these stages for you. Read 'The Ghost at Ivy Cottage' and check what the notes say.

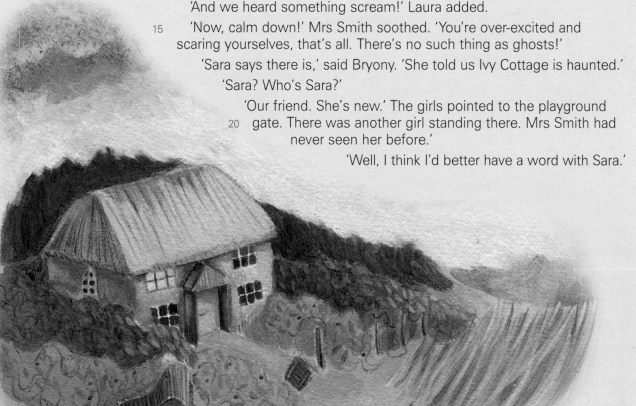

The Ghost at Ivy Cottage

Opening
- Sets the scene.
- Introduces the main character.
- Presents a problem.

It was nearly dusk, and Mrs Smith was walking past the village playing field, when three girls came running out.

'Mrs Smith, Mrs, Smith!' Nicky, Bryony, and Laura were breathless. 'Ivy Cottage is haunted!'

5 Ivy cottage stood on its own on the other side of the field, behind a thick bramble hedge. Mrs Smith looked at the girls in surprise.

'Haunted? Whatever makes you think that?'

Development
- Reveals more about the problem.
- Introduces a new character.

'We saw a light in there!' cried Nicky. 'Through the hedge! But nobody lives there, do they?'

10 'Well, it's for sale, and the people who own it have moved out,' said Mrs Smith. 'Perhaps the estate agent's showing someone round?'

'No, no!' insisted Bryony. 'It wasn't an ordinary light. It was *green* and it flickered.'

'And we heard something scream!' Laura added.

15 'Now, calm down!' Mrs Smith soothed. 'You're over-excited and scaring yourselves, that's all. There's no such thing as ghosts!'

'Sara says there is,' said Bryony. 'She told us Ivy Cottage is haunted.'

'Sara? Who's Sara?'

'Our friend. She's new.' The girls pointed to the playground
20 gate. There was another girl standing there. Mrs Smith had never seen her before.'

'Well, I think I'd better have a word with Sara.'

Complication
- Something happens between the main character and the new character.

Mrs Smith went over to the strange girl, and told her that she shouldn't go round scaring her new friends with silly stories.

25 'But it isn't silly,' said Sara. 'There *is* a ghost.'

'Right,' said Mrs Smith. 'Come with me, and I'll show you you're wrong and there's nothing to be frightened of.'

They all crossed the field. Ivy Cottage was just visible through the dense bramble hedge. There *was* a faint glow in one window, but it 30 wasn't flickering.

'There,' said Mrs Smith. 'It's just an electric light. The owners must be back.'

Crisis
- There is a turning point in the story.

Then suddenly the light turned a cold, strange green, and winked out. At the same moment, a weird cry echoed out of the 35 dusk. Nicky, Bryony, and Laura screamed and ran away. Only Sara didn't run. She just stood staring at Mrs Smith.

'See?' she said.

Resolution
- The reader discovers the answer to the problem.

Mrs Smith was shaken, but collected herself. 'Now stop it,' she said. 'The light bulb went, that's all. And that noise must have been a bird; an 40 owl, probably. There isn't a ghost!'

Sara said, 'Oh, yes, there is.'

She smiled at Mrs Smith. Then, very slowly, she faded away, until there was no one there.

Activity 1

1 Answer these questions to show you understand how 'The Ghost at Ivy Cottage' is structured.

Opening
1 What is the setting?
2 Who is the main character?
3 What is the problem?

Development
4 What more docs the reader learn about the problem?
5 Who is the new character?

Complication
6 What happens between the main character and the new character?

Crisis
7 What is the turning point in the story?

Resolution
8 What is the answer to the problem?

Sharpen spelling

Silent letters

There are few words in the English language that start with the letters *gh*. '*Ghost*' is one of them. When you say the word 'ghost' you do not sound the *h*. It is a **silent letter**.

1 Copy the following words and circle the silent letter(s) in each one.

knee	doubt	wrong
reign	island	pneumonia
know	wreck	psychiatry
gnome	examine	writer
ghetto	definite	debt

2 Check the letters you have circled with a partner. If you disagree, try saying the word:
- pronouncing the circled letter(s)
- not pronouncing the circled letter(s).
Which one sounds correct?

2 Use the five stages and the questions to help you make notes for a ghost story of your own. Copy and complete a table like this to help you.

Stages	Details
Opening: setting, main character, problem	

If you prefer, you could organise your notes under sub-headings:

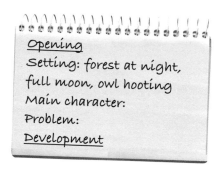

Opening
Setting: forest at night,
full moon, owl hooting
Main character:
Problem:
Development

Or you could use a spider diagram:

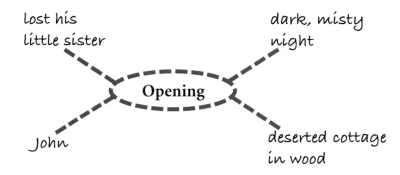

lost his little sister

dark, misty night

Opening

John

deserted cottage in wood

 Feedback

1 Ask a partner if they can work out from your notes what the completed story would be about. They should answer these questions.
  a Do you get a clear sense of what the completed story would be about?
  b Do the five stages of the story do what they should?
  c Is it clear how the story would develop and end?
  d Are any important details or stages missing? If so, what are they?

2 Think about your partner's answers and make useful improvements to your notes.

Story openings

Openings are especially important in stories. They need to be interesting enough to 'hook' the readers and make them carry on reading. Read this opening paragraph of a short story. Then answer the questions that follow.

> The man ran desperately along the road. His heartbeats sounded in his ears in time with his echoing feet on the iron-hard, icy ground. Sweat poured into his eyes though the night was bitterly cold. The headlights of cars going the other way swept past him. No cars seemed to be going his way. His desperation grew.

Activity 2

1 Why do you think the writer says 'the' man rather than 'a' man? What does this tell you about his importance in the story?

2 What do you learn about the setting? Think about:

- place
- time of year
- weather
- time of day.

3 What questions does this opening make the reader want to ask?

4 How does the writer emphasise the man's desperation?

5 What kind of story do you think this is going to be? Explain clearly why you think this.

6 Create your own story opening. Use the idea of a frightened child running through a wood. Write five or six sentences. Aim to describe the setting and 'hook' your reader.

7 Annotate your story opening by using an:
- **S** to point out details of setting
- **H** to point out words or details you have used to 'hook' your reader.

Thinking about the whole story

The paragraph on page 9 comes from a short story called 'Faces'. You are about to read the whole story. The questions between each extract will help you to:

- understand the story
- identify techniques used by the writer.

Faces

The man ran desperately along the road. His heartbeats sounded in his ears in time with his echoing feet on the iron-hard, icy ground. Sweat poured into his eyes though the night was bitterly cold. The headlights of cars going the other way swept past him. No cars seemed to be going his way. His desperation grew.

5   At last, the sound of a car came from behind him. He stepped into the road and into the glare of its headlamps, waving his arms and hardly caring for his safety. The car drew to a halt and the man opened the passenger door.

'For God's sake take me to the next town,' he gasped.

> 1 In lines 11–21 below the writer creates a contrast between the man's desperation and the atmosphere in the car. As you read them:
> - list the details that suggest the car is a safe place
> - list the details given about the driver.

The driver wore a heavy overcoat, a hat pulled low over his face and a
10 woollen scarf.

'Certainly,' he said in a level, smooth, **mellifluous** voice.

For some minutes the journey proceeded quietly. The muffled figure behind the wheel drove speedily along the straight, dark road. His new passenger regained his breath and some of his composure.

15   At length the driver spoke. Once again there could be noticed the calm evenness in his voice.

'Tell me, sir – for indeed I could not help but notice the state you were in when I stopped for you – the cause of your **perturbation**.'

The passenger gulped. For a moment it seemed as though he was unwilling
20 to say anything about his experiences. Then – in the warm, steadily-driven car, insulated from the evils of the dark night outside – he relaxed.

> 2 The writer uses direct speech to reveal what has happened to the man. As the man speaks the writer gives the reader clues that something is wrong. As you read the man's account below, make a note of the clues that tell you something is wrong.

'Very well,' he said.

'My own car broke down about three miles back along the road. I was unable to do anything without help. I realised I was miles from anywhere; no traffic
25 seemed willing to stop for me. It seemed the only course was to walk until I found a house where I might either obtain help or make a telephone call.

'After walking for about half a mile, I saw a house standing back from the road. It was dark, thatched, ivy-covered – seemingly deserted. Nevertheless, it seemed worth enquiring there, in case it was inhabited. Therefore I went up to the front
30 door and knocked at it. To my surprise, it was opened at once.

Word bank

mellifluous sweet, pleasant
perturbation disturbance

11

'In the darkness stood a person – I judged her to be a woman – holding a candle which revealed nothing of her but only the bare floorboards and walls of the entrance hall.

'"Come inside," she said to me.

'The woman beckoned to me and turned away. I followed her. A man's voice,
35 in tones of sweet reasonableness, called from another room.

'"Who is it, my dear?"

'In an equally soft voice, the woman answered, "It is he whom we have expected."

'It was then that I should have run from that accursed place for ever. But I did
40 not. For I felt thankful at having found shelter with people who sounded so pleasant, so kind.

'I was led into a room which once again was in darkness, lit only by faint moonlight which filtered in through curtainless, leaded windows. The shape of a man could be seen standing behind a table, placed on which I could just make out
45 the outlines of an oil lamp. The woman moved away from me to stand beside him.'

3 With a partner talk about:
- the clues you have spotted
- what you think might happen next and why you think this.

Now read on.

'For a moment, there was complete silence and stillness.

'Then the man leant forward. He lit the oil lamp. Its warm, yellow light threw leaping shadows around the room. I looked round at the features of the room now revealed – the beamed ceiling, the oak table, the heavy carved chairs.
50 Then I looked at my new companions, now that I had the light to see them with.

'And then my face froze into horror and my voice formed itself into a wordless scream.

'For the faces of both the man and the woman were the same. No mouth. No nose. No eyes. They were smooth, bare, featureless – as eggs.'

4 Remind yourself what you have learnt about the five stages of a story. What stage do you think is shown in lines 46–54 above? Explain why you think this.

Now finish the story.

55 'Without thinking twice, I turned and ran – out of the house, onto the road, carrying on the way I had been going before; desperate for help, for consolation, for assurance that I had been merely the victim of a mistake, a practical joke, an hallucination, perhaps a nightmare.

'And then, as if in answer to a prayer, you stop for me and I am back in the
60 world of normality.'

He settled back into the front seat of the car as it sped smoothly onward.

The driver's hand stayed calmly on the steering wheel. For the first time since the passenger had commenced his story, he spoke.

'You say their faces had no features on them: they were, in fact, quite blank?'

65 'Yes,' said the passenger.

The driver turned to his companion and with his left hand removed his scarf.

'You mean, like this?'

No mouth. No nose. No eyes. A face as blank and smooth as a featureless egg.

5 How has the writer of 'Faces' surprised his readers? What method does he use in the last line to emphasise the surprise?

6 This story leaves the reader to imagine what happens next.
Talk with a partner about what you imagine happens next.
Do you think this is a good ending? Give at least two reasons for your answer.

Writing for detail

Good writers often give details to help the reader picture what they are describing.

Activity 3

Read the following sentences from 'Faces'. Then write three sentences of your own, creating new details to describe a different driver, house and room.

The driver wore a heavy overcoat, a hat pulled low over his face and a woollen scarf. (Page 11, lines 9–10)

The driver wore ...

'After walking for about half a mile, I saw a house standing back from the road. It was dark, thatched, ivy-covered – seemingly deserted.' (Page 11, lines 27–8)

After walking for about half a mile, I saw a house ...

'I was led into a room which once again was in darkness, lit only by faint moonlight which filtered in through curtainless, leaded windows.' (Page 12, lines 42–3)

I was led into a room which ...

Use of adjectives

One method that the writer uses to build detail and create a clearer picture for the reader is to use adjectives. An adjective is a word that describes somebody or something. The adjectives in the following sentences are underlined.

'Then the man leant forward. He lit the <u>oil</u> lamp. Its <u>warm</u>, <u>yellow</u> light threw <u>leaping</u> shadows around the room. I looked round at the features of the room now revealed – the <u>beamed</u> ceiling, the <u>oak</u> table, the <u>heavy carved</u> chairs.' (Page 12, lines 47–9)

Activity 4

1 Look back at the sentences you wrote in Activity 3.

  a Underline the adjectives you used.

  b Improve the sentences by using *either* a wider range of adjectives, *or* more appropriate adjectives. Here is an example of how you could do this.

>   *cheerful and*   *gleaming, white*
> *I was led into a room that was ~~very~~ bright, as the sun shone through the net curtains.*
>   *golden rays of the morning*

2 Rewrite your redrafted sentences and underline the adjectives in them.
For example:

> *I was led into a room which was <u>cheerful</u> and <u>bright</u>, as the <u>golden</u> rays of the morning sun shone through the <u>gleaming</u>, <u>white</u> net curtains.*

Feedback

1 Decide which of the following statements matches your understanding of adjectives.
- I don't understand how to use adjectives (red light)
- I think I understand how to use adjectives (amber light)
- I understand how to use adjectives (green light)

Mark your work with the colour of the traffic light that matches the statement you have chosen.

2 If you gave yourself a red or an amber light, then you should:

  a re-read the explanation above of what adjectives are

  b copy out the following sentences and underline the adjectives.

    The sparkling red bike.   *Clue: what words are used to describe the bike?*

    The tired old man.   *Clue: what words are used to describe the man?*

    The room was dark and dingy.   *Clue: what words are used to describe the room?*

3 Choose your own adjectives to describe:

  a the bike   b the man   c the room.

Setting and atmosphere

As you have discovered, writers use lots of details to let readers know where a story is set. Re-read the opening paragraph of 'Faces' (page 9). Remind yourself about the kinds of details used to give the setting of a story. Now read the following short story 'A Night at a Cottage' and work through the activities.

A Night at a Cottage

1   What do you learn about the setting in these first few lines? Remember to think about place, time and weather.

On the evening that I am considering I passed by some ten or twenty cosy barns and sheds without finding one to my liking: for Worcestershire lanes are **devious** and muddy, and it was nearly dark when I found an empty cottage set back from the road in a little bedraggled garden. There had been heavy rain
5   earlier in the day, and the straggling fruit trees still wept over it.

2   Good writers create atmosphere in stories. Atmosphere is the mood or feeling that is built up in a story. They do this through the details they give and the words they use to describe them. Here are some of the phrases that the writer has used in lines 1–5 above to create a mysterious and slightly eerie atmosphere.

'it was nearly dark'
'an empty cottage set back from the road'
'a little bedraggled garden'

Copy out this list and add to it by selecting other phrases from lines 6–21 overleaf which help to create atmosphere.

> **Word bank**
>
> **devious** twisting

Word bank

wainscot wooden panelling
haled dragged

But the roof looked sound, there seemed no reason why it should not be fairly dry inside – as dry, at any rate, as I was likely to find anywhere.

    I decided: and with a long look up the road, and a long look down the road, I drew an iron bar from the lining of my coat and forced the door, which was only
10 held by a padlock and two staples. Inside, the darkness was damp and heavy: I struck a match, and with its haloed light I saw the black mouth of a passage somewhere ahead of me: and then it spluttered out. So I closed the door carefully, though I had little reason to fear passers-by at such a dismal hour in so remote a lane: and lighting another match, I crept down this passage to a
15 little room at the far end, where the air was a bit clearer, for all that the window was boarded across. Moreover, there was a little rusted stove in this room: and thinking it too dark for any to see the smoke, I ripped up part of the **wainscot** with my knife, and soon was boiling my tea over a bright, small fire, and drying some of the day's rain out of my steamy clothes. Presently I piled the stove
20 with wood to its top bar, and setting my boots where they would best dry, I stretched my body out to sleep.

> 3 Think of a wood at night. In pairs, build up a list of at least ten
> details that would help to create an eerie, spooky atmosphere.
> For example, *branches like witches' claws.*
>
> 4 As you have seen earlier in this unit, writers give readers clues.
> As you read the rest of the story, try to spot the clues that suggest
> something is not quite right. When you spot them, jot
> down the line number(s) so that you can talk about them later.

I cannot have slept very long, for when I woke the fire was still burning brightly. It is not easy to sleep for long together on the level boards of a floor, for the limbs grow numb, and any movement wakes. I turned over, and was about to
25 go again to sleep when I was startled to hear steps in the passage.

    As I have said, the window was boarded, and there was no other door from the little room – no cupboard even – in which to hide. It occurred to me rather grimly that there was nothing to do but to sit up and face the music, and that would probably mean being **haled** back to Worcester jail, which I had left two
30 bare days before, and where, for various reasons, I had no anxiety to be seen again.

    The stranger did not hurry himself, but presently walked slowly down the passage, attracted by the light of the fire: and when he came in he did not seem to notice me where I lay huddled in a corner, but walked straight over
35 to the stove and warmed his hands at it. He was dripping wet; wetter than I should have thought it possible for a man to get, even on such a rainy night; and his clothes were old and worn. The water dripped from him on to the floor: he wore no hat, and the straight hair over his eyes dripped water that sizzled spitefully on the embers.

40   It occurred to me at once that he was no lawful citizen, but another wanderer like myself; a gentleman of the Road; so I gave him some sort of greeting, and we were presently in conversation. He complained much of the cold and the wet,

and huddled himself over the fire, his teeth chattering and his face an ill white.

'No,' I said, 'it is no decent weather for the Road, this. But I wonder this
45 cottage isn't more frequented, for it's a tidy little bit of a cottage.'

Outside the pale dead sunflowers and giant weeds stirred in the rain.

'Time was,' he answered, 'there wasn't a tighter little cot in the country, nor a
purtier garden. A regular little parlour, she was. But now no folk'll live in it, and
there's very few tramps will stop here either.'

50 There were none of the rags and tins and broken food about that you find in a
place where any beggars are used to stay.

'Why's that?' I asked.

He gave a very troubled sigh before answering.

'Gho-asts,' he said; 'gho-asts. Him that lived here. It is a mighty sad tale,
55 and I'll not tell it you: but the upshot of it was that he drowned himself, down
to the mill-pond. All slimy, he was, and floating, when they pulled him out of
it. There are fo-aks have seen un floating on the pond, and fo-aks have seen
un set round the corner of the school, waiting for his childer. Seems as if he
had forgotten, like, how they were all gone dead, and the why he drowned
60 hisself. But there are some say he walks up and down this cottage, up and
down; like when the smallpox had 'em, and they couldn't sleep but if they
heard his feet going up and down by their doors. Drownded hisself down to
the pond, he did; and now he Walks.'

The stranger sighed again, and I could hear the water squelch in his boots as
65 he moved himself.

'But it doesn't do for the like of us to get superstitious,' I answered. 'It
wouldn't do for us to get seeing ghosts, or many's the wet night we'd be lying
in the roadway.'

'No,' he said; 'no, it wouldn't do at all. I never had belief in Walks myself.'

70 I laughed.

'Nor I that,' I said. 'I never see ghosts, whoever may.'

He looked at me again in his queer melancholy fashion.

'No,' he said. 'Spect you don't ever. Some folks do-an't. It's hard enough for
poor fellows to have no money to their lodging, apart from gho-asts sceering
75 them.'

'It's the coppers, not spooks, make me sleep uneasy,' said I. 'What with
coppers, and meddlesome-minded folk, it isn't easy to get a night's rest
nowadays.'

The water was still oozing from his clothes all about the floor, and a dank
80 smell went up from him.

'God! man,' I cried, 'can't you NEVER get dry?'

'Dry?' He made a little coughing laughter. 'Dry? I shan't never be dry … 'tisn't
the likes of us that ever get dry, be it wet OR fine, winter OR summer. See that.'

He thrust his muddy hands up to the wrist in the fire, glowering over it fiercely
85 and madly. But I caught up my two boots and ran crying out into the night.

5 Take a few minutes to think about the clues you spotted. Talk with a partner about the clues both of you selected. Try to add to your list.

6 Write the answers to these questions.
  a When did you first suspect that the 'stranger' was a ghost? What was it that made you suspicious?
  b Give details of two other clues that made you even more suspicious.
  c When were you certain that the 'stranger' was a ghost? Why?

 Progress check

1 Opposite are the axes for a bar graph. The horizontal line shows what you have studied about stories. The vertical line shows how confident you feel about what you have studied. Copy the axes and complete the bars.

2 Take the two things you feel most confident about. Write one sentence for each, explaining how you think this skill will help you to be a better writer.

3 Take the area you feel least confident about. Using the index below, look back to the pages where the area is covered. Re-read the pages carefully.
Structure of a story, pages 7–9
Story openings page 9
Spotting clues in stories, pages 11–12
Using detail and adjectives, pages 13–14
Creating atmosphere, pages 15–18

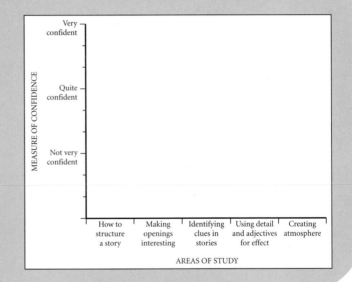

 Sharpen spelling

Groups of silent letters
1 Read the following sentence and identify the words that contain silent letters:
'He gave a very troubled sigh before answering.' (line 53)
2 Try to think of other words that you have not already studied in this unit in which:
  • *igh* is pronounced as i
  • *sw* is pronounced as s
  • there is a silent letter.
Write these words down and underline the silent letters.

Character

A writer can reveal a character to a reader in several different ways, as these examples from 'A Night at a Cottage' show. Answer the questions at the side as you read them.

> He was dripping wet; wetter than I should have thought it possible for a man to get, even on such a rainy night; and his clothes were old and worn. The water dripped from him on to the floor: he wore no hat, and the straight hair over his eyes dripped water that sizzled spitefully on the embers.
> (Page 16, lines 35–9)

A description of the character's appearance
What five details are you given about the man's appearance?

> 'Time was,' he answered, 'there wasn't a tighter little cot in the country, nor a purtier garden. A regular little parlour, she was. But now no folk'll live in it, and there's very few tramps will stop here either.'
> (Page 17, lines 47–9)

What the character says
What does the man know? What does this suggest about him?

> 'There are fo-aks have seen un floating on the pond, and fo-aks have seen un set round the corner of the school, waiting for his childer. Seems as if he had forgotten, like, how they were all gone dead, and the why he drowned hisself.'
> (Page 17, lines 57–60)

The way the character speaks
What is unusual about the way the man speaks? What does this suggest about him?

> He complained much of the cold and the wet, and huddled himself over the fire, his teeth chattering and his face an ill white.
> (Page 17, lines 42–3)

The things the character does
What does this suggest about the man?

> He thrust his muddy hands up to the wrist in the fire, glowering over it fiercely and madly.
> (Page 17, lines 84–5)

What does this tell the reader for certain?

Creating a character

Creating a character needs a lot of thought. Writers will spend a lot of time thinking about the characters in their stories.

Activity 5

1 Study this photograph closely. Talk with a partner about what you think the girl would be like.

2 With your partner, draw a spidergram in which you start to build a character based on this photograph.

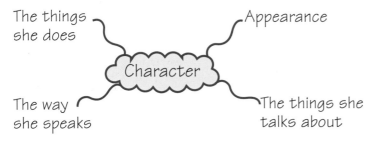

Dialogue

To create an interesting story, writers often use a mixture of:
- action – the events of the plot
- description – of setting and character
- dialogue – the words the characters actually say.

As you have seen, the ghost in 'A Night at a Cottage' (pages 15–17) reveals important details from the past when he speaks.

Activity 6

1 When writing dialogue you need to make it easy for the reader to follow. Read the following extract. Use your knowledge of writing dialogue to:
   a work out why this extract is difficult to follow
   b list the things you would need to do to make it easier to follow.

> But it doesn't do for the like of us to get superstitious, I answered. It wouldn't do for us to get seeing ghosts, or many's the wet night we'd be lying in the roadway. No, he said; no, it wouldn't do at all. I never had belief in Walks myself. I laughed. Nor I that, I said. I never see ghosts, whoever may. He looked at me again in his queer melancholy fashion. No, he said. Spect you don't ever. Some folks do-an't. It's hard enough for poor fellows to have no money to their lodging, apart from gho-asts sceering them. It's the coppers, not spooks, make me sleep uneasy, said I. What with coppers, and meddlesome-minded folk, it isn't easy to get a night's rest nowadays. The water was still oozing from his clothes all about the floor, and a dank smell went up from him. God! Man, I cried, can't you NEVER get dry? Dry? He made a little coughing laughter. (lines 66–82)

2 In your list in **1b** you should have included these things:
- start a new line each time a person starts to speak
- put inverted commas " " at the beginning and end of the words that are spoken.

There are other rules for the presentation of direct speech but the two listed above are the most important. Try to explain why.

3 Rewrite lines 66–82 so that they are easier for the reader to follow. Remember to:
- set out the speech correctly
- use inverted commas around the words that are spoken.

4 You, or a partner, can check your work against lines 66–82 on page 17. Start with a total mark of 20. Take off 1 mark:
- if you have not started a new line when you should
- if you have not used inverted commas where you should have done
- if you have used inverted commas where you did not need to.

If your final mark is less than 14, you need to look back through this activity.

Sharpen punctuation

Inverted commas

1 Can you think of other times when you would need to use inverted commas in your writing? List them.

2 Rewrite the following sentences using inverted commas in the right places.

a She was reading The Lord of the Rings when her friend came to see her.

b Turn right and then left, the passenger told the driver.

c According to the story the man made a little coughing laughter when he was asked about getting dry.

Comparing stories

It is useful to compare the ways that different stories are written. You are going to compare the openings and endings of the three stories you have read in this unit.

Comparing openings

Activity 7

1 Look at page 22 and remind yourself of the openings of the three stories you have read in this unit: 'The Ghost at Ivy Cottage', 'Faces' and 'A Night at a Cottage'.

It was nearly dusk, and Mrs Smith was walking past the village playing field, when three girls came running out.

'Mrs Smith, Mrs, Smith!' Nicky, Bryony, and Laura were breathless. 'Ivy Cottage is haunted!'

Ivy cottage stood on its own on the other side of the field, behind a thick bramble hedge. Mrs Smith looked at the girls in surprise. (lines 1–6)

From 'The Ghost at Ivy Cottage'

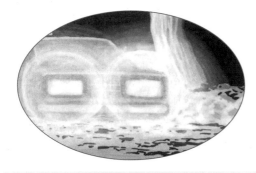

The man ran desperately along the road. His heartbeats sounded in his ears in time with his echoing feet on the iron-hard, icy ground. Sweat poured into his eyes though the night was bitterly cold. The headlights of cars going the other way swept past him. No cars seemed to be going his way. His desperation grew. (lines 1–4)

From 'Faces'

On the evening that I am considering I passed by some ten or twenty cosy barns and sheds without finding one to my liking: for Worcestershire lanes are devious and muddy, and it was nearly dark when I found an empty cottage set back from the road in a little bedraggled garden. There had been heavy rain earlier in the day, and the straggling fruit trees still wept over it. (lines 1–5)

From 'A Night at a Cottage'

2 Copy and complete this table to show the ways in which the story openings are similar or different.

Feature	'The Ghost at Ivy Cottage'	'Faces'	'A Night at a Cottage'
First character introduced is the main character		Yes: the frightened man	
Written in first person (I, we) or third person (he, she, it, they)	Third person: 'Mrs Smith was'		
Time		the night	
Weather			'heavy rain earlier'
Written in which tense		Past: 'The man ran'	
Place	'Ivy Cottage stood on its own on the other side of the field, behind a thick bramble hedge'	The road (but 'dark, thatched, ivy-covered' house later on)	

Comparing endings

Writers will always try to give the best possible ending to their story.

Activity 8

1 Remind yourself of the endings of the three stories in this unit.

Mrs Smith was shaken, but collected herself. 'Now stop it,' she said. 'The light bulb went, that's all. And that noise must have been a bird; an owl, probably. There isn't a ghost!'

Sara said, 'Oh, yes, there is.'

She smiled at Mrs Smith. Then, very slowly, she faded away, until there was no one there. (lines 38–43)

From 'The Ghost at Ivy Cottage'

The driver's hand stayed calmly on the steering wheel. For the first time since the passenger had commenced his story, he spoke.

'You say their faces had no features on them: they were, in fact, quite blank?'

'Yes,' said the passenger.

The driver turned to his companion and with his left hand removed his scarf.

'You mean, like this?'

No mouth. No nose. No eyes. A face as blank and smooth as a featureless egg.

(lines 62–8)

From 'Faces'

The water was still oozing from his clothes all about the floor, and a dank smell went up from him.

'God! man,' I cried, 'can't you NEVER get dry?'

'Dry?' He made a little coughing laughter. 'Dry? I shan't never be dry … 'tisn't the likes of us that ever get dry, be it wet OR fine, winter OR summer. See that.'

He thrust his muddy hands up to the wrist in the fire, glowering over it fiercely and madly. But I caught up my two boots and ran crying out into the night.

(lines 79–85)

From 'A Night at a Cottage'

2 With a partner talk about the ways in which these endings are similar and different. Use details from the text to support the different points you make. It will help you to think about:

● what use the writers make of dialogue

● when the true identity of the other person is revealed

● how the true identity of the other person is revealed

● what you learn about the main characters' feelings

– before they discover the truth

– after they discover the truth.

3 Write a paragraph (between five and eight sentences) pointing out the similarities and differences between the endings of the three stories. Here are some suggestions to help you put your ideas into sentences.

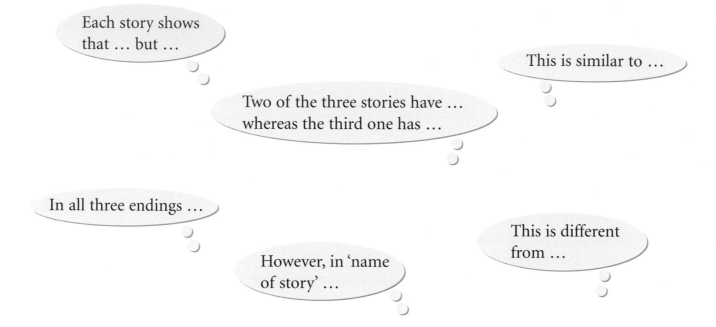

Each story shows that … but …

This is similar to …

Two of the three stories have … whereas the third one has …

In all three endings …

This is different from …

However, in 'name of story' …

Your response

Now that you have explored all three stories, think about your own response to them.

Activity 9

1 On your own, decide which story you most liked. Think of and list as many reasons as you can for your choice. Your list:
- should include references to particular things you liked in your chosen story
- might include reasons why you didn't like the other stories as much
- might include details of how the story made you feel at different times in it.

2 Find someone else in your class who liked the same story as you. Share the reasons for your choice. Aim to build up a set of convincing reasons. It's not enough to say 'It's really good' or 'The ending works well'. You need to explain what makes it 'really good' and why the 'ending works well'. Remember to use details from the text to support the points you make.

3 Present your ideas to a larger group or to the whole class. Remember to:
- make your points clearly
- support them with examples from the texts.

Assessment task

Spooky Tales

Dreadful deeds. Harrowing horrors.
Menacing mirages.

Join us in our search for the spookiest tale of all!

Entries should be between 250 and 750 words.
All tales will be judged by our reader panel.

Follow the spooky trail

 The first thing you need to do is get some good ideas.
Think about the following and jot down your ideas.

Where could your story take place?

deserted cottage
graveyard
wood
park
church
castle
somewhere else

When would it take place?

night-time
dusk
morning
mid-day
ten years ago
a hundred years ago
some other time
now

Who is the main character?

man   woman   girl   boy

What does the main character look like?
What kinds of things would they do?
What kinds of thing would they say?
What other things could you say about them?

Who or what is 'the spook'? Is it somebody
returned from the dead? Or is it something else?
What does 'the spook' look like?
What kinds of things would 'the spook' do?
What kinds of things would 'the spook' say?
What other things could you say about 'the spook'?

What is going to happen?
Where will your story start?
What kinds of things could happen?
How could these things be resolved?

 Once you have gathered lots of ideas,
sort through them and pick out the
best ones. Try to avoid:

- having too many characters in your
  story – two or three is enough
- making your story too unbelievable
  – your reader needs to be
  convinced this is really happening.

Cross out the ideas that are not helpful.

 Highlight thinking

Checking and refining solutions
It is important to sift through your
thoughts and ideas. This will help you
get your best result.

Here you are gathering ideas, choosing the
best ones, putting your thoughts in order
and making decisions. You are drafting and
checking your work, acting on feedback
from others and making improvements.

Think about where else you might use
these skills.

 Decide on the order in which things are
going to happen. It might help if you copy
and complete a table like the one on page 27. Or you could make
notes under the sub-headings: opening, development, complication,
crisis, resolution.

Stages	My ideas
Opening What is going to happen at the start? Give the setting through place, time and weather. Introduce the main character. There may already be a problem.	
Development What is going to happen next? You might introduce your 'spooky' character, though it might not be clear yet that there is anything wrong.	
Complication How do your main character and 'spooky' character meet? What happens between them? Do they talk to each other? Do you show anything new about them from the ways they talk?	
Crisis What happens to bring the story to a turning point?	
Resolution How does the story end? What different things are made clear to the reader?	

a Think about possible opening and closing sentences for your story. Write down two or three possible sentences for each before you decide on the best ones.

b Think about words you could use to create a spooky atmosphere. Jot down at least ten words and/or phrases before moving on to the next step.

c Decide whether you are going to write your story in the first person (I, we) or the third person (he, she, it, they).

Write the first draft of your story. Remember to:
- use the past tense
- organise your ideas into paragraphs
- give descriptive detail
- include correctly set out dialogue
- frequently re-read what you have written to check it makes sense.

When you have finished and checked your first draft, exchange your story with two or three other students in your class. Ask them to tell you:

- two things they think are good about your story
- two things they think you could improve.

Make sure you keep a record of what they say.

Improve your story, taking into account the comments of the people who read your first draft. Here are some of the things you may need to do:

- Cross things out that don't make sense.
- Add more descriptive detail.
- Change your opening or ending to make it more exciting.
- Change the order of events so that you don't give too many clues too soon.

Here is an example of redrafting. The black print shows you how it was to start with. The red print shows you the changes that have been made to improve it.

,misty   dimly   starless
It was a dark ˅night. The moon shone ˅in the ˅sky.
A   was
~~There was a~~ ˅man ˅walking down the road ~~and he was~~ looking for
in the distance.
somewhere to stay. He saw a castle ~~ahead of him~~ ˅~~and~~ Although
knew he
it looked really eerie and creepy, ~~but~~ he ˅had to stay somewhere
decided he would give it a try.
and he ˅~~went there to see if they would let him stay there.~~

Re-read your redrafted story closely.

- Is there anything else you could do to make it better?
- Could you include more spooky adjectives?
- Do you need to check any spellings in the dictionary?

When you are completely happy with it, make a neat copy.

Before your final copy is ready you need to proofread it. This is the stage where you check it thoroughly and correct any errors in spelling and/or punctuation. Look out for the things you know you often get wrong. For example:

- using *of* when you should use *have*:

  He could ~~of~~ *have* escaped through the window.

- missing out apostrophes:

  The stranger wouldn't say what his name was.

- using a comma when you need a full stop:

  The cold rain hit the woman's face. She turned and walked away.

Ask a partner if they can spot any errors that you have missed.

Have fun reading as many of your class's Spooky Tales as you can!

2 Ways with words

The bigger picture

In this unit you will think carefully about how to use the right words in the right places. You will explore how writers use different words for different purposes and learn how to adapt the words you use. At the end of the unit you will make a presentation to your class about improving your classrooms.

WHAT? You will:
- explore the ways in which you use words
- practise using formal and informal words
- investigate how choice of words affects meaning
- examine the use of pictures in texts

HOW? by:
- working out what kinds of words are used in a range of texts
- understanding the difference between spoken and written language
- choosing the best words to match the purpose of your text
- making the connection between words and pictures in texts

WHY? because:
- it will help you understand how writers match their words to the type of text they are writing
- to be a good writer you need to be able to adapt your words to the text you are writing
- by using words and pictures together you will learn how to make an impact on your readers

How do we use language?

We use language every day, most of the time without thinking about it. Thinking, speaking and using a wide range of vocabulary are as automatic to us as breathing or eating.

Activity 1

1 Work with a partner to make a list of the different purposes of language. Set out your answers in a table like the one below. Allow yourselves ten minutes to think of as many examples as you can.

Purpose of language	Example
To give explanations	Explaining to a teacher why your homework is late
To entertain	Telling a joke to a friend

2 When you have finished, share your ideas as a class. Listen carefully to the ideas of other students so that you can add to your own lists.

3 a Consider these statements about language and decide whether you agree, disagree or are not sure about them.

Little children always speak English badly.

The Queen speaks better English than we do.

People judge you by the way you speak.

We speak differently when we are with our friends.

News readers have to speak English very well.

Girls speak better than boys.

b With a partner talk about the statements. Begin by comparing which statements you agree or disagree with and why you hold this opinion. Use the connectives in the box below to help you give your explanations.

because   as   so   for example   because of this   however

Make sure that you:
- give several reasons to support your ideas using the connectives in the box
- help your partner to think of ideas.

c Work with your partner to write one sentence about each statement to explain your thinking. For example:

> Little children always speak English badly.
>
> We disagree **because** it is very difficult to speak English properly and **as** little children are only learners they are bound to make some mistakes.

Make sure you both write your sentence down.

d Share your ideas with the rest of the class by reading out your sentences.

Working out meaning

Benjamin Zephaniah is a poet who enjoys using words. Read the poem 'For Word' on the next page carefully and you will see why.

Activity 2

1 His poem 'For Word' also shows that the *sounds* of words in poetry are very important. Read this poem aloud with a partner so you can enjoy the sound of the words.

2 Work out exactly what Benjamin Zephaniah is saying about words. Copy out the ideas below, then find a quotation from the poem that matches each one.

The effect of the words on the poet	Matching quotation
Make him feel happy	Thanks for words that make me smile
Make him feel sad	
Prove a point	
Allow him to be creative	
Allow him to appreciate sounds	
Explain his thoughts	
Give him pleasure	
Communicate with other people	

FOR WORD

🌢 **Thank you** for the *words* I read
Thank you for the **words** I need
Thank you for the WORDS so great
Thanks for *words* that raise debate,
5   Thanks for the **words** on my bookshelf
Thanx for the *words* I make myself
Thank you for the words that make me cry
And words that leave me feeling dry.

❝ **Thanks** for WORDS that do inspire
10   And those **words** that burn like fire
Thanks for all the *words* I note
Thank you for all the *words* I quote,
I thank you for the **words** like me
Thanks for *WORDS* that set me free
15   And I thank you for *words* like you
I always need a word or two.

🌙 **Thanks** for words that make things plain
And **words** that help me to explain
Thanks for *words* that make life fun
20   And *words* that help me overcome,
Thanks for **words** that make me rap
Thanks for words that make me clap
Thanks for *WORDS* that make me smile
Thanks for WORDS with grace and style.

25 ☞ **Thanks** for all those **words** that sing
Thanks for words are everything
Thanks for all the **WORDS** like this
And little sloppy *words* like kiss,
Thanks for **words** like hip-hooray
30   And those cool words I like to say
Thanks for *words* that reach and touch
Thank you very, very much.

Benjamin Zephaniah

Sharpen spelling

Vowel sounds

In line 18 the poet uses the word 'explain'. The two vowels – *ai* – make a long vowel sound. A long vowel is one where two vowels have the same sound as the name of the first letter.

1   *ai* makes a long vowel sound in the **middle** of words. Copy these words, filling in the missing letters: excl _ _ m   dr _ _ n   str _ _ ghten
    Think of at least three other words that use *ai*.

2   The long vowel *a* sound is made at the **end** of a word by the letters *-ay*, for example: *day, sway, stray*.
    Think of at least three other words like this.

Commenting on the writer's choice of presentation

Being able to understand and explain the choices writers have made is an important skill.

Activity 3

To help you understand the choices Benjamin Zephaniah has made in his poem, copy and complete the sentences below. You may find it useful to talk about the answers with a partner before you write them down.

- When I first saw the poem on the page, I was _____ .
- The writer has used _____ different fonts in this poem. I think he has done this because _____ .
- The poet has made every stanza begin with a different symbol. This makes the poem look _____ .
- In the first stanza the poet has altered the spelling of 'thanks'. The reason for this could be _____ .
- I think the poet chose to present his poem like this because _____
  _____ .

Writing your own poem

You will notice two important things about the poem 'For Word'.

- Every pair of lines rhymes. Lines that rhyme like this in pairs are known as rhyming couplets.
- The words 'thank you' or 'thanks' are repeated at the beginning of almost every line. This gives the poem a special rhythm or beat. The rhymes at the end of each line also help to give the poem its rhythm or beat.

Activity 4

Write your own poem called 'Words', using rhyme and rhythm in the same way as Benjamin Zephaniah has done. Follow the steps below. Aim to write at least six lines. Your poem should have:

- at least six ideas about words arranged in rhyming couplets
- some lines that begin with the words 'thanks' or 'thank you'
- a strong rhythm or beat where sounds are emphasised.

Step 1
Make a list of reasons why you might feel grateful for words. Look back at the work you did on the purposes of language on page 31 to get some ideas. Arrange your ideas in a spider diagram, for example:

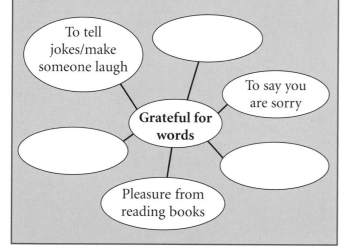

Step 2
Take one of your ideas and experiment with rhymes for it, for example: *laugh / bath.*

Step 3
Now put your ideas and rhymes into two lines, for example:

Thanks for words that make me laugh
Even when I'm in the bath

- Carry on building up your lines like this until you have written your poem.
- You will find it helpful if you read your poem aloud as you write each pair of lines. This will help you to build a good rhythm into your poem.
- You can tell whether or not you have the right rhythm by reading your lines aloud to see if you can hear the beat.

Highlight thinking

Spider diagrams
It's useful to use a spider diagram to:
- get ideas down quickly without sequencing them or deciding which are most important
- spark off new ideas because your mind will make associations from one idea to another
- see the central idea and your different ideas around it visually, at a glance.

Step 4
Think about the presentation of your poem.
- How could you write the title to make it look attractive for your readers?
- Which words do you want to write in a different font to draw attention to them and to make your poem fun to look at on the page as well as to read aloud?

Feedback

1 Show your poem to a partner. Read it aloud to them or get your partner to read it aloud to you so that you can hear what it sounds like.

2 Ask your partner to help you assess your work. Give your poem a score of 1 (needs a bit more work), 2 (good) or 3 (excellent or very good) to each of these features:
   - ideas
   - using words in rhyming couplets
   - creating a good rhythm
   - making your poem look attractive on the page.

3 Copy and complete these sentences using your own ideas and the feedback from your partner to help you.

> I am very pleased/pleased/quite pleased with my poem.
>
> The parts I liked the most were _____ because _____ .
>
> The areas I need to improve on are _____ because _____ .

Formal or informal?

Have you noticed that you probably talk to your friends and your teachers in different ways? We change the way we speak depending on who we are speaking to and why we are talking to them. Some of the differences between formal and informal language are shown in the tree diagram below.

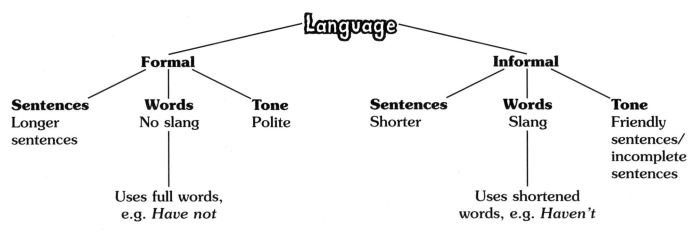

Language

Formal

| **Sentences** | **Words** | **Tone** |
| Longer sentences | No slang | Polite |

Uses full words, e.g. *Have not*

Uses polite form of address, e.g. Mr, Sir, for example:
Could you come this way please, Sir?

Informal

| **Sentences** | **Words** | **Tone** |
| Shorter | Slang | Friendly sentences/ incomplete sentences |

Uses shortened words, e.g. *Haven't*

Uses Christian names and nicknames, for example:
That was really wicked, wasn't it Nicky?

Highlight thinking

Tree diagrams

It's useful to use a tree diagram when:

- you are working with known facts or features. You can display how they relate to each other – such as the 'rules' of formal or informal language
- there is a logical path to follow. For example, if you are using formal language then it follows that you won't use slang. A tree diagram will help you choose the right feature.

Activity 5

1 With a partner look at the list below. Decide which of the conversations are formal and which are informal.

- A mother telling a young child not to do something and explaining why not.
- A boss interviewing a candidate for a job.
- A teacher asking students to explain why they are out of class during lesson time.
- A pet owner teaching a puppy how to cross the road.
- Someone persuading a friend to stay at their house for the weekend.
- A policeman interviewing a motorist about driving too fast.

2 Work with a partner to improvise one formal conversation and one informal conversation from the list. Each conversation should last for about two minutes.

Remember, improvise means to make something up without preparation – you do not need to write anything down.

Feedback

1 Ask another pair of students to listen to you while you perform your improvisations. Use the diagram on page 36 to help you answer these questions:
   a Which conversation was informal? Which conversation was formal?
   b How could you tell? Give examples.

2 Now listen to another pair perform their improvisations.

3 You will have worked out by now that there are clear differences between formal and informal talk. Imagine that you have to explain these differences to someone who is younger than you. Write four short sentences to explain the differences.

4 Show your sentences to a partner to check how clear and accurate they are. Would a younger reader understand your explanation? Revise your explanation in light of your partner's comments.

Speech and writing

Now that you have worked out the difference between informal and formal talk, you are going to look at the differences between speech and writing.

 Activity 6

1 Carefully read the texts below.

Text A
This is a transcript (written record) of a conversation between two friends.

SAMMY	Hey, guess what?
KERRIS	What?
SAMMY	We're getting a new kitten!
KERRIS	You lucky—
SAMMY	He's dead cute. We went to see him last night.
KERRIS	Where—
SAMMY	Er – that cat rescue place in Silverbottom.
KERRIS	Cool!

Text B
This extract is from a magazine article.

My best friend

I know it's a cliché to say dogs are a man's best friend, but in my case it's true. Sampson my Golden Retriever has been with me for ten years since he was a beautiful golden-haired bundle of fun, the cutest puppy I had ever seen.

One of my favourite Saturday morning activities is a walk – or more accurately a run – on the beach with Sampson. His tail starts to wag as soon as we approach the beach.

2 Copy and complete this table to help you work out the differences between speech and writing. Make sure you give examples from the texts.

Text	Uses mainly full sentences	Uses mainly one word or incomplete sentences	Records the way we hesitate when speaking	Uses formal vocabulary/ standard English	Uses informal vocabulary/ slang words
Text A (Conversation)			Er		
Text B (Magazine article)				cliché, accurately	

3 To revise what you have just learnt, write three or four sentences about the differences between speech and writing.

4 Show your sentences to a partner and ask them to check that you have included all the main points. Then check your partner's work. If you have missed anything out, revise your sentences to include it.

Considering audience

Just as speech can be formal or informal depending on the speakers and their purpose for speaking, so can writing. Writing can change in formality according to the purpose and the audience.

 Activity 7

1 Read review A below and review B on page 40. Answer the questions around them.

This is the language of everyday speech. How many more examples can you find?

Review A

Times Newspapers Ltd, 2003

2 FAST 2 FURIOUS

☆☆☆☆☆ 12

Put your foot on the gas and enjoy the high-revving action of 2 Fast 2 Furious as street drivers Paul Walker and Tyrese infiltrate a money-laundering businessman's dealings. The plot is hardly supercharged (it's plain predictable) but the Miami location, slick race action and cool cars make it a whole lot of fun. Overall, this is prime-time popcorn viewing where the cars are the stars.

What does the writer mean by this phrase?
Why is it a good phrase to use in this review?
Think about the audience.

Review B

> ## 2 FAST 2 FURIOUS
> ### Cert. 12   4/5
> This is an ideal video to keep your children entertained on a wet Sunday afternoon. The plot, set in Miami, is an innocuous tale of money laundering. However, the real stars of this film are the cars and the most gripping scenes take place on the race track. This video is definitely good value for money as your children will want to watch it over and over again.

 Is this word formal or informal? Why has it been used here? Think about the audience.

> ❝ **Sharpen punctuation**
>
> **Commas**
> Read the following sentence from Review B. Can you explain why the words *set in Miami* are placed within commas?
>
> > The plot, set in Miami, is an innocuous tale of a money laundering.
>
> **1** Copy and complete these sentences by adding your own information between the pairs of commas.
>
>   a John, _____ , scored the winning goal.
>
>   b London, _____ , is visited by thousands of tourists every year.
>
>   c The dog, _____ , helped to catch a burglar.

2 Now think about the similarities and differences between Review A and Review B.

  a Which review is formal and which is informal? How can you tell?

  b Who is the audience for the first review? What are the clues?

  c Who is the audience for the second review? What are the clues?

 Writing your own review

A review informs someone about a book, CD, film and so on. The reviewer also gives their opinion of the item they are reviewing.

Activity 8

1 Write your own review of a book or a film you have enjoyed. Write in an informal style for readers your own age. Aim to write about eight lines. Before you begin, remind yourself of the main features of reviews listed on the next page.

When you write a review:
- Write in the present tense.
- Begin with an opening statement which states your point of view clearly.
- Use positive language to persuade your readers to read the book or see the film.
- Provide some details about the book or film.
- Use facts to support your opinions.
- Remember to keep your audience in mind when you write. In this review, use the sort of informal language that young people will feel comfortable with.
- Finish with a repetition of your opening statement.

 **Highlight thinking**

Flowcharts

It is useful to use a flowchart to:
- sequence your ideas – make sure that you write in the order that is best for your purpose
- structure your ideas – make sure that you have planned what you want to say, and where.

A flowchart might help you plan your review. You could include the points listed on the left.

2 Ask a partner to check that your review has all the features as listed in the box. Edit your work in light of your partner's feedback.

 Progress check

Look back at the learning you have done so far in this unit. You have:
- thought about how you use language
- shared your ideas with other students
- used appropriate connectives when giving explanations
- thought about how language is used to entertain readers and make them think
- worked out the differences between formal and informal language
- worked out the differences between speech and writing
- improvised formal and informal conversations with a partner
- revised the use of commas in pairs
- revised the features of writing to review.

1 Which two things on this list do you feel you have done best? Write them down and draw a star by them.

2 Which two things do you think you need to learn more about? Write them down and draw an arrow beside them. For each one, write a sentence explaining why you feel unsure about it.

Presenting information texts

The presentation of a text refers to the way it is set out on the page. Writers present their texts in different ways according to their:

- **purpose** (the reason for writing)
- **audience** (the people who will read them).

Activity 9

Look at the four information texts below and on page 43. Identify the audience and purpose for each one and then copy and complete the following table.

Text	Audience	Why I Think this	Purpose	Why I think this
A				
B			to give directions	
C				
D	friend			

Text A

Text B

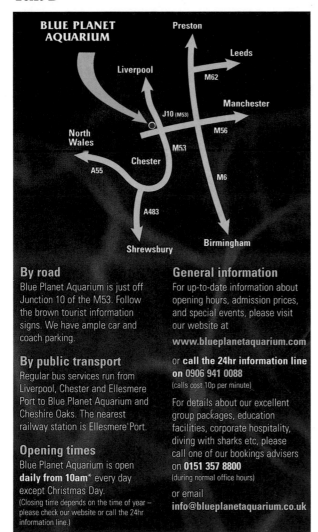

By road

Blue Planet Aquarium is just off Junction 10 of the M53. Follow the brown tourist information signs. We have ample car and coach parking.

By public transport

Regular bus services run from Liverpool, Chester and Ellesmere Port to Blue Planet Aquarium and Cheshire Oaks. The nearest railway station is Ellesmere Port.

Opening times

Blue Planet Aquarium is open **daily from 10am*** every day except Christmas Day.
(Closing time depends on the time of year – please check our website or call the 24hr information line.)

General information

For up-to-date information about opening hours, admission prices, and special events, please visit our website at
www.blueplanetaquarium.com

or **call the 24hr information line on 0906 941 0088**
(calls cost 10p per minute)

For details about our excellent group packages, education facilities, corporate hospitality, diving with sharks etc, please call one of our bookings advisers on **0151 357 8800**
(during normal office hours)

or email
info@blueplanetaquarium.co.uk

Text C

Environmental Development Services
129 Dawson Road
Greenport
GP1 3JT

Planing Consultation   22 August 2004

The Owner/Occupier
29 Waddington Road
Greenport
GP3 6RO

Dear Sir/Madam

I am writing to inform you that I have received a planning application that affects land close to your address. If you wish to look at the plans and supporting documents, please call at the Council Offices at the opening times given on the attached leaflet.

Yours faithfully

B. Robson

B. Robson

Text D

Understanding presentational features

You will remember that a presentational feature is something which draws attention to a text. Think about the different presentational features that you have come across so far.

Activity 10

1 Copy this spidergram and add your own ideas to it.
2 Look at the list of presentational features on page 44. Add any features you have missed to your spidergram.

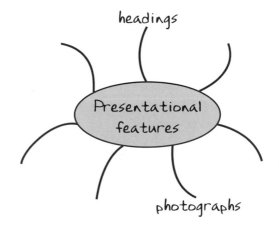

Presentational features

- Addresses.
- Writing organised into paragraphs.
- Headings and subheadings to organise information.
- Short sentences in list form.
- Use of alternative spelling/shortened words.
- Different font sizes/styles for headings and important information.
- Different types of print, for example: bold, italic, capitals.
- Logos.
- Pictures and captions.
- Maps or diagrams.
- Colour for background and lettering.

3 You will notice that Texts A–D on pages 42–3 are presented differently, according to their purpose. Which features on the list are used in each text?

Choose three features and explain why you think the writer has chosen to use them. Remember the connectives you have used so far for explaining – *because, so, as.*
For example:

> Text C has a logo at the top of the letter because the writer wants the reader to know the letter has come from the local council and that it is a formal, official letter.

Using presentational features

Look closely at the information on teeth below. It has been written for younger children and its purpose is to inform. The writers have finalised the words, but have not added any presentational features.

Activity 11

1 Using the features listed above decide how to make it look more interesting.

2 Copy the text, adding presentational features to it to help readers understand the information more easily.

Teeth: fascinating facts

Did you know ...?

The biggest tooth in the world belongs to the sperm whale. Its bottom jaw consists of one huge tooth that can measure up to 5 metres long.

Lemon sharks get a whole new set of teeth every two weeks.

Rabbits' teeth never stop growing.

Teeth are amazing ...

They are covered in the hardest substance in your body. This is known as enamel. Just think, if you did not have teeth you would not be able to chew or bite food.

Look after them; they're precious.

Everybody has bacteria in their mouth which feed on the sugars left behind after you have eaten. The acids created by the bacteria can make holes in your teeth. This is known as tooth decay. To help fight tooth decay you should brush your teeth at least twice a day, preferably with fluoride toothpaste.

Feedback

1 Assess your partner's work. Use the following questions as a guide for assessment and award a mark of 1 (needs a bit more work), 2 (good) or 3 (excellent or very good).
   - Have they used a range of presentational features?
   - Have they presented the text in the most effective way to inform?
   - Will the presentation appeal to younger children?

2 Explain the marks you have given your partner.

3 Ask your partner to explain the marks they have given you.

4 Record the marks your partner gave you. Write down two ways in which you could improve your use of presentational features.

Formal language in information texts

Information texts sometimes need to be written in formal language.

Activity 12

1 Read the letter on the right. What is the purpose of the letter and who is the audience?

2 Write down three features that show you that it is written in a formal style. Look at:
   - the vocabulary
   - the type of sentences (long/short, simple or complex)
   - the tone of the letter.

3 Look at the information in the Blue Planet leaflet on pages 46–7. The first time you read the leaflet you should **skim** read it. Then talk with a partner about the contents of the leaflet.

> Waterside Primary School
> Larkspur Lane
> Wigan
> WG9 2QP
>
> The Publicity Officer
> Blue Planet Aquarium
> Ellesmere Port
> Cheshire
> CH6 5LF
>
> Dear Sir/Madam
>
> I am the teacher of a Year 6 primary class. We are currently studying life under the ocean and I would like to bring my pupils to the Blue Planet Aquarium to extend their knowledge.
>
> Please could you let me know what experiences you offer to school parties? I would be very grateful for a prompt reply.
>
> Yours faithfully
>
> *J Jefferson*

4 You are going to write a reply to the letter above using information from the Blue Planet leaflet. To find the information you need you will scan the text. Scanning means moving your eyes quickly over the page until you find the information you need you are looking for. The best way to scan a text is to look for key words. Follow steps 1–5 on pages 46–7 to write your letter.

It's the closest you'll get

New for 2003

Meet the **otters!**

Our new otter enclosure is one of the largest in the UK. Otters are amongst the most delightful of creatures and you'll rarely get to see them in the wild.

Close encounters

What does it feel like to stroke a dogfish? Is a ray hard or soft to the touch? Young and old will be spellbound by our rockpools with their friendly inhabitants.

Amazing views

The spectacular 230ft-long Aquatunnel with its moving walkway takes you through the depths of our huge Caribbean reef. There are hundreds of fish of all types in specially-themed habitats throughout Blue Planet Aquarium.

Pretty deadly!

Don't be fooled by the vivid colours of some frogs – they can contain enough poison to kill several humans!

Step 1: Make notes

Copy these headings and use the key words to help you find the information you need in the text. Then make your own notes under each heading. An example has been done for you under the first heading.

1 **Rare/unusual water creatures**   Key words: *rarely, largest*
   Otters – rarely see them in the wild

2 **What you can see**   Key words: *spectacular, awesome, amazing*

3 **What you can touch**   Key words: *touch, stroke*

4 **Of special interest to a school party**   Key words: *so much to do*

without getting wet!

Blue Planet Aquarium is Britain's Ultimate Underwater Adventure and features one of the world's longest underwater viewing tunnels. You can get right up close to huge sharks, graceful rays and hundreds of other amazing fish in realistic surroundings. It's a great day out, whatever the weather – and an experience you'll never forget.

Huge sharks

Blue Planet Aquarium is home to one of Europe's largest collections of sand tiger sharks. At 10ft (3m) long, they are simply awesome! Will you dare take your eyes off them?

So much to see and do!

Make sure you don't miss a thing! Look out for the times of shows in the Aquatheatre. One of our marine biologists will tell you about the amazing fish swimming past the huge window and you can also see divers hand-feeding the sharks.

Take a break in our super Caribbean Restaurant – but make sure you've got enough time to browse round the gift shop, which stocks a large selection of toys, books and mementos to suit all pockets.

The Arapaima is the world's largest freshwater fish... and we've got the biggest in the UK!

Step 2: Plan your letter

Copy this table and make notes in the spaces to help you plan your letter.

Opening paragraph – How I will begin my letter: Explain to the teacher why you are writing.	
Paragraph 2 – Information I will include: Use your notes from the first three headings and decide the order in which you will use them.	
Paragraph 3 – My next set of information: Use your notes from heading 4.	
Concluding paragraph – How I will end my letter: Show that you are willing to help with further enquiries.	

Step 3: Write the first draft of your letter
Using your plan, write the first draft of your letter. Remember to:
- write in paragraphs
- sound polite and helpful
- use formal language.

Step 4: Revise your letter
a Working with a partner check that you have:
- used four paragraphs
- included all of the relevant information
- used formal language.

b Read your letter aloud to your partner to check that it makes sense. Do you need to alter the order of any sentences, or make them shorter or longer to improve your letter?

c Check for spelling mistakes, and correct use of capital letters, full stops and commas. Mark all of the corrections on your letter.

d Finally, read the letter again to make sure you have included all necessary changes.

Step 5: Write the final version
Now write the final draft of the letter and include all the changes.

✓ Progress check

1 Write down answers to the following questions. Since the last progress check you have:
   a explored how writers present their texts in different ways. They consider two things before choosing how to present texts. What are they?
   b revised the use of presentational features in an information text. Name five features.
   c used the skills of skimming and scanning to find information. When would you use each skill?
   d used formal language in a letter. What three key things should you remember?

2 Swap your answers with a partner and award one mark for each right answer. If you need to check an answer, the page numbers listed below will point you in the right direction.

Question a: Page 42   Question c: Pages 45, 47
Question b: Page 44   Question d: Page 48

Check your progress!
1–4 marks   You understand some things about presentation and information texts. Check which questions you lost marks on. Refer back to the pages listed above, then try the questions again.

5–9 marks   You are doing well. Which questions did you lose marks in? Refer back to the pages listed above to refresh your memory.

9–12 marks   Congratulations! An impressive score.

Words and images

You have been studying how writers use language and different presentational features to give information to readers. Now you are going to look at texts where only a few words and images are used to make an impact on readers.

Look closely at this appeal, which appeared on the front of an envelope for the charity *Save the Children*.

Activity 13

1 With a partner discuss these questions.
   a   What did you notice first – the words or the pictures?
   b   What would make you open the envelope to look inside?

2 Describe the expression on the child's face. Why do you think the advertisers chose this photograph?

3 Why do you think the designers placed the slogan at the side of the advertisement and not in the middle?

4 What is the purpose of the strip that runs along the bottom of the envelope?

Now look at the back of the envelope.

5 Why do you think the designers put a photograph of a child on the back of the envelope?

6 Write down the slogans on the front and back of the envelope. What is the difference between them?

7 What do you think this appeal is trying to make readers:
   • feel   • do?

Taking a closer look

The text you are about to study uses even fewer words to get its message across.

Activity 14

1 Study the poster below and answer the questions around the text.

1 What did you notice first about this advertisement?

2 Why did the designers place the picture of the boy's face at the top?

3 What does branded mean? How does it link with the picture?

4 How does the slogan help you to understand the picture?

5 What is the purpose of this text?

6 What will you remember most about this advertisement?

2 Copy and complete these sentences to help you work out the effect the words have on the reader.

> a The writer uses the word 'branded' with a double meaning. The two possible meanings of 'branded' are: _____ and _____ .
>
> b The writer has used the word 'branded' here because they want the reader to realise that _____ .
>
> c The writer also uses the word 'bang' with a double meaning. In this advertisement the word 'bang' could mean _____ or _____ .
>
> d 'Bang' is a good word to use in this advertisement because it will make the reader think _____ .
>
> e 'Fool' is not a very polite word. I think the writer has used it in this advertisement because _____ .

Design your own poster

You have now learnt how to achieve an impact in your writing and presentation. So it's time to have a go for yourselves.

Activity 15

1 Work with a partner on the *first draft* of a poster warning about the dangers of fireworks. Your purpose is to make your readers think. Your ideas and your design are more important than producing a polished poster.

Follow these guidelines.
- Use one large picture to gain your readers' attention (a sketch is sufficient).
- Use one warning written in large letters.
- Use one simple but clear message at the end.
- Use a slogan.

2 Show your poster to another pair in your class. Explain why you have chosen your image and slogan. Use these prompts to help you explain:
- the impact you want your poster to make. For example, you might want it to warn or shock your readers.
- why you chose your images.
- why you think your slogan will be effective.

Ask your class to feed back on the impact of your image and the way you have used words to get your message across.

✓ Progress check

1 Explain how words and pictures together can have a powerful effect on the reader of a charity appeal.

2 Write down two things you have learned about the importance of using pictures in a poster intended to give a warning message.

3 Write down two things you have learned about the power of words in a poster intended to warn.

Presenting your ideas

You've just looked at a poster which gives a warning. You can also use a poster to display your ideas and help in giving a presentation.

You are going to work in pairs or groups of three to:
- study and comment on information about texting
- decide how to present your ideas to a larger group.

Read these facts on text messaging:

Fact File

📱 In the UK we send a billion text messages a month.

📱 As many as one in four young people might have been bullied by texts or e-mail.

📱 Text messaging has created a new global language.

📱 Teachers have been given clear rules by the government on how to handle text bullying.

📱 A headteacher is introducing extra English lessons because he says text messaging is affecting the way his students write.

📱 Children who text while crossing the road are at great risk of being killed in a traffic accident.

📱 A teenager got into trouble after writing an English essay in the style of a text message.

Activity 16

1 Talk about the facts and what you think about each one. One person needs to make notes.

2 Decide which facts are most interesting. Choose three or four and highlight your comments on these in the notes.

3 Now add to these comments, for example:

Our comments:
I've been bullied by text and it's very upsetting

Add:
One way to stop this is . . .

4 You are going to present your ideas on a poster and through talk. Decide who will prepare the talk and who will prepare the poster. Read the hints before moving on.

Hints: preparing your poster
- Remember that the purpose of your poster is to present your ideas so that they can be easily understood.
- Choose an eye-catching title.
- Use colours, large letters and pictures to make your comments stand out.
- Make sure people can read your comments.

Hints: presenting your talk
- Decide who will speak and in which order.
- Speak loudly and clearly.
- Try not to turn your back on the audience as you point things out on your poster.

 Feedback

1 As you listen to the presentations of other groups, award a mark of 1 (needs a bit more work), 2 (good) or 3 (excellent or very good) for each of the following features:
- a display that is interesting to look at
- ideas that are explained clearly and in detail
- a team presentation, in which everyone has something to say
- voices that are loud and clear.

2 Collect your scores from the audience and discuss them as a group.

3 Write down two targets for improving speaking/presentation skills that your group can work on.

Assessment task

Present your ideas!

- Work in groups of three.
- You are going to make a five minute presentation to the School Council on your ideas for improving classrooms in your school.
- You may make your presentation either on a poster or using a multi-media approach.
- You will be expected to explain your ideas using formal language.
- Follow steps 1–4 below.

Step 1: Gather your ideas

1 Think about how you will divide up the jobs in your group. Your group will need someone to:
   - lead the discussion, keep everyone on task and make sure you finish all the tasks on time
   - make notes on what you discuss
   - report back to the rest of the class.

2 With your group, think about the classrooms in your school. Talk together about your answers to these questions.
   - What are the important features of good classrooms?
   - What do you like about the classrooms in your school? Make a list of all the reasons you like these rooms.
   - Which classrooms don't you like? Why? What improvements do they need?

   Write two or three sentences to sum up your ideas.

3 Now think about your ideal classroom. What should it have to help students learn comfortably and safely? Discuss and make notes about:
   - colours you would like
   - the type of furniture you would like
   - wall decorations, including noticeboards
   - computers and other learning aids
   - anything else that would make learning easier and more comfortable.

4 Now report back to another group and share your ideas so far. Listen carefully to the ideas of the other group, as you may be reminded about something you have forgotten.

5 Review your ideas. Have you got enough material for a five-minute presentation? Do you need to add anything?

Step 2: Plan your presentation

1 Remind yourself of the success criteria for this assessment:

Success criteria for this assessment task

- Use a loud, clear, confident voice.
- Use appropriate connectives to explain your ideas.
- Use formal language.
- Explain your ideas in detail.
- Use visual aids to support your presentation.
- Persuade your audience by your choice of words and pictures.

---

2 Decide the following:
- how you will start
- the order in which you will present your ideas
- how you will finish.

3 Think about how to present your ideas visually. You could produce a poster or a PowerPoint slide. Include designs for your ideal classroom.

Step 3: Rehearse your presentation
Practise your presentation until you are confident.

Step 4: Present your ideas
Remember to present your ideas in a clear and confident voice. Ask the class to feed back three strong points and three suggestions for improvement after the presentation.

 You have worked hard for this presentation. Enjoy it!

3 Poetry power

The bigger picture

In this unit you will explore how writers use a range of techniques to express their ideas in poetry. At the end of the unit you will explain how two poets have used some of the techniques you have explored.

WHAT? You will:
- consider how poets shape meaning
- explore poetic techniques such as alliteration, imagery, rhythm and rhyme
- develop your ability to plan and write interesting poetry

HOW? by:
- reading poems from different times and cultures
- exploring the effects achieved by poets using a variety of techniques
- writing your own poems using these techniques

WHY? because:
- by reading different poems you will become more familiar with the range of poetic techniques and be able to explain how poets use them
- making links with the poetry you read helps you to write interesting poetry
- expressing ideas in poetic form will help you to develop your own writing skills

Exploring poetry

In this unit you will read and write a variety of poems.

Activity 1

1 a Begin by thinking about what poets do. In what ways do you think they are similar to or different from other kinds of writers like novelists or journalists?

   b Read 'Poem for a Dead Poet' on page 58. As you read it, look for descriptions of what the writer says that poets do.

2 At the end of the poem the writer says that poets almost make words talk. Write down two more things the writer says poets do.

3 Read 'Reader: But what is Poetry?' on page 58 in which Adrian Mitchell writes about many aspects of poetry. As you read, look for ideas about poetry which you feel you understand and can explain.

4 Working on your own, copy and complete the table below. Select three ideas from the poem which you feel you understand and can explain. An example is given.

Example	Idea	Explanation
'Poetry tunnels you out of your dungeon.'	Poetry can help you escape from your own little world into other worlds.	Sometimes we feel trapped – like in a prison – and probably a bit down. Poems can help us to escape from these feelings by taking us into happier worlds. If you're feeling unhappy you might read a funny poem which could make you smile.

Poem for a Dead Poet

He was a poet he was.
A proper poet.
He said things
that made you think
5 and said them nicely.
He saw things
that you or I
could never see
and saw them clearly.
10 He had a way
with language.
Images flocked around
him like birds,
St Francis, he was,
15 of the words. Words?
Why he could almost make 'em talk.

Roger McGough

Reader: But what *is* Poetry?
Adrian:

Poetry is a beautiful mud-pie
Washed down with a glassful of stars.

Poetry is one of the best ways
Of singing to the whole wide world
5 Or whispering in the ear of your
best friend.

Poetry tunnels you out of your dungeon.
Poetry captures the three-headed dragon.
And teaches it Ludo and Frisbee-throwing.

10 Poetry is a Mammoth in a shopping mall,
A beggar with no legs in Disneyland,
A chocolate bicycle,
A truthburger with French flies
And the Moon's own telephone.

15 Poetry is your own mind dancing
To the drumbeat of your heart.

Adrian Mitchell

5 When you have finished, show your table to a partner. Discuss your ideas and explanations. You don't have to agree. In fact, it will be more interesting if you respond in different ways to the poem.

6 Choose one of your examples and give a brief report to the class. You might use the following prompts.
- I have chosen …
- I think that the poet is suggesting that …

When you have listened to what others in your class have said about the poem you should have a range of different explanations of the main ideas in the poem. Write down three of your ideas about the poem.

7 Now write your own poem about poetry. Read the following four lines, which are from a longer poem called 'Poetry' by Eleanor Farjeon.

> What is Poetry? Who Knows?
> Not a rose, but the scent of the rose;
> Not the sky, but the light in the sky;
> Not the fly, but the gleam of the fly;

To explain poetry, the poet describes what makes things special: the 'scent' of the rose, the 'light' of the sky and how flies 'gleam'. To say things 'nicely', as Roger McGough says in his poem (line 5), Eleanor Farjeon uses rhyme: 'Knows / rose' and 'sky / fly'. Write four lines that could follow the four lines already given from 'Poetry'. Approach it in the following way.

a Choose something and describe its special quality in one line, for example, 'Not the car, but the zoom of the car.'

b Think of another idea. Check that you can make a rhyme with your first idea. For example: 'Not the guitar, but the music of the guitar.'

c Repeat these stages and write another two lines.

How poets organise ideas

Activity 2

Think about how Adrian Mitchell has organised his ideas in 'Reader: But what is Poetry?' on page 58. It will help you to explore the poem in more detail. With a partner, decide whether the following statements about the poem are true, false or partly true.

a The poem is written in the present tense.

b Every stanza begins in the same way.

c The stanzas grow in length as the poem develops.

d The poem rhymes.

e Each line has approximately the same number of syllables.

Looking at the same subject in a different poem

Now you are going to look at another poem about poetry. It makes some similar points about poetry but is written in a very different way.

Activity 3

1 Read 'Poetics' by Benjamin Zephaniah on the next page. As you read, think about how it is similar to and different from 'Reader: But what is Poetry?'. Note down these similarities and differences, for example:

SIMILAR	DIFFERENT
Both poets think there is a great variety of feelings in poetry.	Benjamin Zephaniah's poem is much longer than Adrian Mitchell's poem.

2 Share your ideas with a partner. Explain where you found your evidence for the list of points you have made. Help each other to organise your list into three sections.

> What is similar and different in the two poems?
>
> IDEAS
>
> LANGUAGE
>
> ORGANISATION

POETICS

There's a poem on your face
There's a poem in the sky
There's a poem in outta space
There are poems passing by,
5 There are poems in your dreams
There are poems in your head
Sometimes I cannot get to sleep
Cause there are poems in me bed.

There are poems in me tea
10 There are poems on me toast
I have found much poetry
In the place I love the most,
There's a poem right in front of you
Get to know its rhyme,
15 If you are not sure what to do
Just call it poem time.

There's a poem in me shoes
There's a poem in me shirt
When the poem meets the blues
20 It can really, really hurt,
Other poems make you grin
When they dribble off your chin
Some poems think they are great
So they like to make you ...

25 **Wait**
I see poems in your teeth
I see poems in me cat
I hear poems underneath
Going rata tat tat tat,
30 This one has not finished yet
It keeps coming on the beat
It is soggy and it's wet
But it's also very sweet.

There are poems for the **ear**
35 There are poems for the page
Some poems are not quite clear
But they get better with age,
There are poems for the hip
There are poems for the hop
40 Everything is poetic
Poetry will never stop.

There are poems on your **fingers**
There's a poem on your nose
If you give it time to linger
45 It will grow and grow and grow,
There's a poem in you beautiful
Can't you see it
It's right

There,
50 I think it's so incredible
There   are   poems
Everywhere.

Benjamin Zephaniah

Using rhyme

Activity 4

1 Now write your own poem of four lines in a similar style to 'Poetics'. Take the same subject: 'There are poems everywhere'. Use rhyme in the same way as the poet. Choose one of the following phrases to start your poem:

There's/There are ...

I see/hear ...

Or you could try a different sense:

I touch/smell/taste ...

The example below shows you how one writer was thinking as he wrote:

> **What rhymes with 'garden'? – the last two letters of 'kitchen' or a word like 'bin'?**

> I smell poems in me (garden)
> I smell poems in me school
> (Even) in the rubbish (bin)
> Poems can be cool.

> **Use 'bin' but also need 'Even' to draw attention to how a rubbish bin is very different from a garden. Poetry isn't always about 'lovely' things like flowers.**

Think ahead in the same way as you write your poem.

2 When you have finished your poem, write it down. Around it, put your thinking in thought bubbles to show:
   a   the ideas you were describing
   b   the alternatives you thought about when choosing rhyming words.

A poem from long ago

Poetry has been with us for many centuries. Although the language in older poems may be a little unfamiliar, you will recognise many of the same techniques that you see in modern poetry.

Activity 5

1 'I Had a Dove' was written in the nineteenth century by John Keats. Five words have been missed out of the poem. As you read it, work out what those words might be. Copy the table on the next page, write the words in it and say why you have chosen those words.

I Had a Dove

I had a dove and the sweet dove [1]_____;
And I have thought it died of grieving:
O, what could it grieve for? Its feet were [2]_____,
With a silken thread of my own hand's weaving;
5 Sweet little red feet! why should you die –
Why should you [3]_____ me, sweet bird! Why?
You [4]_____ alone in the forest-tree,
Why, pretty thing! would you not live with me?
I kissed you oft and gave you white peas;
10 Why not live sweetly, as in the green [5]_____?

John Keats

When you are choosing your words, think about:
- how the rhyming pattern helps you to decide on a word
- the 'clues' you get from the words around the missing word
- the rhythm that comes from the way the words are arranged in a line.

Number	Word to be inserted	Reason
1		
2		
3		
4		
5		

2 Discuss the words you chose with a partner. Listen to why your partner chose their word. Decide between you which is best and why.

3 There are four question marks in the poem. The dove might give the same answer to all four questions. What do you think the answer will be?

4 Write the dove's reply to the 'I' character in the poem. Write:
- *either* four lines in which the first two lines rhyme with each other and the third and fourth lines rhyme with each other
- *or* four lines in which the first and third lines and the second and fourth lines rhyme.

Try to have about eight or nine syllables in each line. Remember, syllables are the units of sound in a word. In line 2 of 'I had a Dove' there are nine syllables: And / I / have / thought / it / died / of / griev / ing.

Feedback

1 When you have finished, swap your poem with another student. Give feedback on how successful you think their poem is. Comment on:
   a whether the poem rhymes according to one of the suggested patterns
   b whether the rhyming words make sense or have been chosen only because they sound the same
   c whether the poem makes sense as a response to the original poem in which the dove died because it was kept in captivity.

2 Think about the feedback you received on your poem and make improvements.

5 Because 'I Had a Dove' was written in the nineteenth century, you would expect to find some examples of an older form of English.
   a Make a list of the words or phrases that show the poem was written a long time ago.
   b List anything else about the poem that makes it seem as though it was written a long time ago.

Playing with language

Sometimes poetry can seem strange, not because the words are old-fashioned, as in the poem 'I Had a Dove' (page 63), but because of the ways in which the poet 'plays' with language. Read the following poem.

Spell

A clip of thinder ever the reeftips
sends like a bimb going iff!
My hurt thimps in my chist.

It's dirk. The clods are block with reen.
5 The wand blues in the trays.
There's no mean.

I smuggle ender my blinkets
and coddle my toddy.
Sloop will have drums in it.

Carol Ann Duffy

The writer has slightly changed the spellings of several words. Notice how she usually changes the vowels, rather than the consonants.

Activity 6

1 In pairs, use this information to work out the correct words for the first line. Begin with 'thinder'. If the vowel 'i' is incorrect, what must that word be?

2 Now work out the 'correct' spelling for all the 'wrong' words in the poem. Write out a complete 'correct' version.

3 Why do you think the title of the poem is 'Spell'?

4 Some of the writer's changes create other proper words, for example, 'clip' in line 1. Other words such as 'bimb' (line 2) do not exist.
  a   Find three examples of changes that lead to proper words.
  b   Find three examples of changes that lead to non-existent words.

5 Carol Ann Duffy changes the spelling of words and creates a strange, magical atmosphere. Something similar happens in Shakespeare's *Macbeth*, when the three witches chant a magic spell. Read the following section of the spell.

Sharpen spelling

Homophones

Homophones are words that sound identical but are spelled differently, for example: *bear* and *bare*, *moose* and *mousse*, *sight* and *site*.

1 Write down five pairs of homophones.

2 Use each pair of homophones to write two lines of rhyming poetry. For example:

When you're having a shower and you are bare
You really don't want to meet a grizzly bear.

Fillet of a fenny snake,
In the cauldron boil and bake;
Eye of Newt, and toe of frog,
Wool of bat and tongue of dog,
5 Adder's fork and blind-worm's sting,
Lizard's leg and howlet's wing,
For a charm of powerful trouble,
Like a hell-broth boil and bubble.

Macbeth, Act IV, Scene I

6 a Re-write Shakespeare's spell, using the same technique as Carol Ann
Duffy in 'Spell'. Change vowel sounds and also some consonants if you
feel it makes words that sound interesting. Make pairs of lines rhyme.
For example, you might begin:

Figget of a funny snook
In the cooldrun bail and book

b When you have finished, read your spell aloud to a partner.

Investigating poetic techniques

You may already have learnt about different poetic techniques.
The main ones are:

- similes
- metaphors
- personification
- alliteration
- rhythm
- rhyme

Activity 7

1 Try to give an example of each technique, using the following statements to
match your understanding.

- I don't know what this
  means.
- I think it means …

- I know it means …

I am not very confident
about this aspect.

I'm well on the way to a good
understanding of this.

I'm very confident about my
ability to explore this aspect.

2 Now work through pages 66–70, which will explain these techniques in
more detail. (So don't worry if you scored some ambers and reds.)

Similes, metaphors and personification

Activity 8

1 In pairs, discuss how a little boy could be like a kite.

Similes and metaphors involve a kind of comparison. With **similes**, the
comparison is direct and the word 'like' or 'as' is used. In this example, the
writer uses 'as' to compare a boy to a kite.

> Fragile as a kite
> over the roofs of Barrancas
> little Luchin was playing

From 'Luchin' by Victor Jara

With **metaphors**, the comparison is implied or suggested. In this example, the writer compares a tiger to fire.

> Tyger! Tyger! Burning bright
> In the forests of the night

From 'The Tyger' by William Blake

2 In pairs, discuss how a tiger could be like fire.

In many metaphors the suggested comparison invites the reader to compare objects with humans or living things. This is called **personification**.

> I remember, I remember,
> The house where I was born,
> The little window where the sun
> Came peeping in at morn.

From 'I Remember, I Remember'
by Thomas Hood

3 In pairs, discuss how the sun is personified. What opinion of the sun is suggested by the personification above? Does the sun sound like something pleasant or unpleasant?

4 a On your own, read the lines of poetry below. Decide whether they give examples of similes, metaphors or personification.
   b Write down why you think each writer made these particular comparisons.

> Freezing dusk is closing
>   Like a slow trap of steel
> On trees and roads and hills and all

From 'The Warm and the Cold' by Ted Hughes

> It is the end of a school day
>   and down the long drive
> come bag-swinging, shouting children.
>   Deafened, the sky winces.
> 5   The sun gapes in surprise.

From 'At the End of a School Day' by Wes Magee

> sweat sliding down
> his muscly mahogany face

Describing a West Indian preacher in
'Be a Butterfly' by Grace Nichols

5 Share your notes from question 4 with a partner. Discuss each set of lines in turn.

    a Do you agree on the answers?

    b Do you think your partner's ideas about why the writer used that comparison are clear and as fully explained as possible? For example, in 'Like a <u>slow</u> <u>trap</u> of <u>steel</u>' do they explain each of the underlined words?

6 Now experiment with some poetry of your own, focusing on making comparisons. Choose a person you know well – perhaps a parent, brother, sister or friend. Write a poem in which you describe this person in a list of similes and/or metaphors. You need to think about the different aspects of the person you could describe, for example:

    a appearance

    b behaviour/manner/attitudes

    c other things about them, such as the way they move.

Remind yourself of the work you did earlier on how poets structure their ideas in poems. Use **6a**, **b** and **c** as three sections of your poem. Think about each one in turn. For example, for **a** you might write something like: 'My mum's eyes are brown like shades of autumn' (a simile). For **b** you might write: 'She whirlwinds round the house when angry' (a metaphor).

Write at least three comparisons for each of the three sections.

Beware of using clichés in your writing. Clichés are phrases that have been used so often they become stale and boring. Many similes are clichés. You will have heard phrases like 'cool as a cucumber' and 'red as a beetroot' before. Try to be imaginative with the comparisons in your own similes. Avoid using comparisons you have heard before.

 Highlight thinking

Making comparisons

It often helps to look at something from a different angle. You can use your imagination to put very different things together because they have *some* similarities. Using comparisons can help you to:

- think creatively and see connections between things or ideas that seemed completely unconnected
- make your writing more powerful. Instead of stating something about a character such as 'she was vicious', you use comparison with other things that are 'vicious'. 'She snarled' uses a comparison with a dog to *suggest* viciousness.

Feedback

1 Swap your finished poem with a partner. Think back to the kinds of observations you made about the similes in the poems on page 67–8, when you looked at and explained comparisons. Think about the following points and write a brief commentary on your partner's poem.

   a Does the poem include similes and/or metaphors?

   b Are the similes interesting? Choose one that seems to be particularly interesting and explain why you think it is good.

   c Is the list of comparisons in a random order or can you see that your partner has tried to organise the list in some way?

2 Read your partner's comments. Discuss how you might improve your poem.
   - rewrite some lines to make sure they contain a simile or a metaphor
   - change some of your comparisons because they might be clichés or because your partner might suggest they are not very effective
   - change the order of your list so that you group similar aspects of the person together.

Alliteration

Poets use alliteration for two main reasons.

Reason 1: to draw attention to particular parts of a poem. For example, in 'Praise of a Collie', a poem about a sheepdog, Norman MacCaig writes:

> Once gathering **sh**eep on a **sh**owery day

The repetition of *sh* draws attention to the two key words in the line: 'sheep' and 'showery'.

Reason 2: to capture a particular sound. For example, in 'The Highwayman', Alfred Noyes writes:

> Over the **c**obbles he **c**lattered and **c**lashed in the dark innyard.

The poet uses a hard *k* sound at the start of 'cobbles', 'clattered' and 'clashed' because he is trying to capture the hard sound of footsteps on a stone yard.

Activity 9

1 Read the following examples of alliteration. Identify the repeated sound and write a brief explanation of why the writer might have used it.

> Shock-black bubble-doun-beat bouncing

Linton Kwesi Johnson

> I hear lake water lapping with low sounds by the shore

From 'The Lake Isle of Innisfree' by W B Yeats

2 Write a short poem of six lines that uses alliteration to capture sounds in a fresh and interesting way. Your poem will be about school. The steps below may help.

Step 1

Begin by thinking of and listing some school situations in which you are aware of hard and soft sounds. Think of suitable vocabulary for these situations. You could use a dictionary and a thesaurus to help you.

Step 2

Choose three letters (or combinations of letters like *cl* or *tr*) from the alphabet which you think are 'hard' sounds. Then choose three letters (or combinations of letters) which are 'soft' sounds.

Step 3

Write three lines about school in which you use alliteration to capture 'hard' sounds, using a different letter sound on each line. Then write three lines in which you use alliteration to capture softer sounds. Here is an example of each.

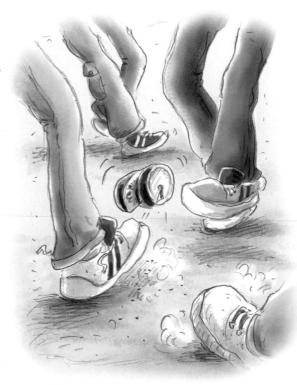

Kids kick clattering cans around

The hard sound of *k* is used.

Silently students stare at test papers

The softer *s* is used to emphasise the lack of noise.

3 Share your lines with a partner. Work together to combine your two lists of school situations into one poem.
- Your poem will be in two sections: one about loud noises and one about softer noises.
- You may decide to use *all* the lines you have *both* written. Alternatively, you can select the best lines from both poems and leave out the ones you feel don't sound right.

✓ Progress check

Look back at the learning you have done so far in this unit. You have:
- thought about the different ways of interpreting the **ideas** in poems
- studied how poets choose to **organise** their ideas
- looked at some of the ways in which **poems from long ago** are different
- considered the ways in which poets **play with the sounds** of words
- examined different **techniques used** by poets, for example: similes, metaphors, personification and alliteration.

Read the following poem and answer the questions that follow it. Answering the questions will help you to decide how confidently you are able to use the skills you have been developing.

Meeting at Night

The grey sea and the long black land;
And the yellow half-moon large and low;
And the startled little waves that leap
In fiery **ringlets** from their sleep,
5   As I gain the cove with pushing **prow**,
And quench its speed **i'** the slushy sand.

Then a mile of warm sea-scented beach;
Three fields to cross till a farm appears;
A tap at the pane, the quick sharp scratch
10   And blue spurt of a lighted match,
And a voice, less loud, thro' its joys and fears,
Than the two hearts beating each to each!

Robert Browning

Word bank

ringlets little curls of hair
prow the front end of a boat
i' a shortened form of 'in'

1 This poem tells a story. In a few words, what is the story it tells? (**Ideas**)

2 Why do you think the writer organised the poem into two sections? (**Organisation**)

3 What are the clues in this poem that tell you it was written a long time ago? (**A poem from long ago**)

4 Which words does the poet use to capture sounds? (**Playing with language**)

5 Are there any examples of alliteration in the poem? Why do you think the writer has used them? (**Poetic techniques**)

6 When the writer describes the waves, what technique does he use? (**Poetic techniques**)

Match your answers with those given by your teacher. Give yourself a red, amber or green light for each of the five aspects of poetry you have explored so far:

Red: I am not very confident about this aspect.
Amber: I'm well on the way to a good understanding of this.
Green: I'm very confident about my ability to explore this aspect.

Rhythm and rhyme

When we speak, our voices go up and down. We stress some parts of words more than others. Think about names. When they contain two syllables we stress one syllable more than another – usually the first one, for example:

KA / ren   LE / roy

When there are three or more syllables, something similar happens:

Ra / JIN / der   STEPH / an / ie

Activity 10

1 Write out the following names in the same way, making the stressed syllables stand out in larger letters.

David Beckham   Leonardo DiCaprio

Martin Luther King   Florence Nightingale

Poets sometimes organise words so that there is a pattern of stressed and unstressed syllables. These patterns are often the first thing we notice about some poems. When we read or say poetry we notice the following things.

- The words are recited in a special rhythm that makes the words sound different from 'ordinary' language.
- There is a often a pattern of rhymes (or words at the end of lines that sound the same).

For example, words like these are usually spoken in a particular way:

> Georgie, Porgie pudding and pie
> Kissed the girls and made them cry.

When we say these words aloud, we recite them in a particular way. The words don't really seem to mean very much. What we notice is the rhythm:

> GEOR - gie, POR - gie PUDD - ing and PIE
> KISSED - the - GIRLS and - MADE - them - CRY.

The pattern of stressed and unstressed syllables is:

> TUM-ti TUM-ti TUM-ti-ti TUM
> TUM-ti, TUM -ti, TUM -ti, TUM.

2 Use the names of students in your class to write two lines that imitate this pattern. For example:

SUzie, BRITney, ROBert and SAM
MAry, DELroy, ROBBie, ROSE

3 Next, add rhyme. Make a two-line list of something in the same rhythm but this time make the lines rhyme. You could use either your own ideas or the ideas below.

fruits   drinks   names

countries   place names

Here are two examples to help you get started:

In this example using vegetables, the two rhyming words are full rhymes. The vowel sounds *ee* and the following consonants *ns* are identical:

Parsnips, carrots, turnips and beans
Marrows, peas and winter greens.

In this example using football teams, the vowels do not sound the same. There is a *u* sound in one word and an *i* sound in the other, but the final consonants are the same. This is called consonantal rhyme:

Arsenal, Bolton, Chelsea and Hull
Reading, Charlton, Leeds, Carlisle.

4 Read your two lines aloud to a partner and check the following.
- Do the lines rhyme?
- Do your two lines in the pattern have stressed and unstressed syllables:

TUM-ti TUM-ti TUM-ti-ti TUM
TUM-ti, TUM -ti, TUM -ti, TUM.

The two lines you have written will probably have very little meaning. You will have concentrated on choosing words that match the rhythm and that give you rhyme.

Look at the next example:

England, Scotland, Ireland and Wales
Winter storms and howling gales.

These two lines rhyme, there is a pattern of stressed and unstressed syllables, and there is an idea in them – they say something about the weather in the UK. Once the first line had been written and ended in 'Wales' the writer had to find a rhyme for that word, and that shaped the second line.

5 Work with a partner. Write a second line to follow 'England, Scotland, Ireland and Wales' that *doesn't* end with the word 'gales'. The topic does not have to be the weather.

   a Begin by making a list of words that rhyme with 'Wales' to help you decide what your second line will be.

   b Read your two lines aloud to the rest of the class and listen to what other pairs have written.

6 Rhythm and rhyme help to make poetry stand out from 'normal' words and make it memorable. Centuries ago, before many people could read or write, stories were often told using lots of rhythm and rhyme to help make them memorable. You will know that Shakespeare uses both rhythm and rhyme in his plays. One of the things that makes rap so popular today is the way rap artists use very strong rhythms and rhymes.

Bringing rhythm, rhyme and similes together

Read the following extract from the poem 'Wurd Up' by Martin Glynn. The poet is writing about using rhythm and rhyme.

From Wurd Up

I'tz time
Ter climb
'n' rime
The sign
5 Just growz
'n' flowz
'n' showz
'n' throwz
a skill
10 Ter thrill
'n' kill

Jus chill
Coz
I'm
15 Stingin like a nettle
Jus bitin like a flea
Smoother than a baby's skin
Much ruffer than the sea
Colder than an icicle
20 Hotta than the sun
Lirix always on the move
Like bullets from a gun

Martin Glynn

Activity 11

1 There are several instances in the poem of words being spelled in unusual ways.

   a With a partner, look at these words and jot down some ideas about why they are written in this way.

   b Does the rhythm – the beat – of those lines change? Where?

2 The poet entertains by using a rhyme several times, for example: *skill / thrill / kill / chill*. He draws attention to the rhyme by having very short lines so that the rhymes appear quickly after one another.

    a Choose your own topic and rhyming sound, and write a similar series of lines. You might start with a word and see where it takes you. Or you might decide on a topic first and then try to find lots of rhyming words that suit the topic. Here is an example that comes from the word 'bees' and ends up being about a picnic:

    b Martin Glynn uses rhythm, rhyme and a series of comparisons to write about the power of words (for example, 'Stingin like a nettle'). Look at how he uses comparisons and rhymes as well as keeping a rhythm in the last eight lines of the extract.

> **Picnic**
> Bees
> Buzz through trees
> In the breeze
> Whilst auntie's
> 5 Knees
> Freeze.

3 Use 'Wurd Up' as a model for writing your own poem. You could choose your own subject, but if you can't think of one, choose a person you know well. Here is an example that follows the same rhyme scheme as Martin Glynn's poem:

> **My Sister**
> Dances like a puppet
> Sings like a night cat
> Gets angrier than a pit bull
> Is sneakier than a rat
> 5 More gormless than a muppet
> Colder than a frozen pool
> But she's my sister and
> I think she's really cool.

Remember, your objective is to experiment with language so that you:
- use rhyme in a pattern
- write lines that can be chanted aloud in a rhythm
- use comparisons
- write an entertaining poem by putting all of the above together.

    a Write a first draft of your poem. When you get stuck – you might be struggling to find a rhyme – ask a partner to help you.

    b When you feel your poem matches the four objectives listed above, write a final draft and read it aloud to either a small group or the whole class.

Showing your understanding of poetry

Poems are written for many reasons. Sometimes they express strong feelings held by the poet. You may be asked to show your understanding of the poet's feelings.

Activity 12

1 Read 'Talking Turkeys' on the opposite page by Benjamin Zephaniah. When you have finished, jot down your first impressions about:

a the subject matter of the poem

b the poet's attitude towards this subject

c anything interesting you notice about the language.

2 Re-read the poem a stanza at a time. Decide on a brief sub-heading or label for each stanza to help you see how the writer has organised their thinking. Make a note of any words or lines you find difficult.

3 Many words are spelled in ways that are not standard, for example: 'yu', 'dis', 'dem'. Consider the following possible reasons for this and decide which is best.

a The poet can't spell very well.

b The spellings show the way the poet speaks and this is his own honest voice.

c The poem isn't meant to be taken seriously, so the poet plays around with spellings.

Talking Turkeys

Be nice to yu turkeys dis christmas
Cos' turkeys just wanna hav fun
Turkeys are cool, turkeys are wicked
An every turkey has a Mum.

5 Be nice to yu turkeys dis christmas,
Don't eat it, keep it alive,
It could be yu mate, an not on
    your plate
Say, Yo! Turkey I'm on your side.

I got lots of friends who are turkeys
10 An all of dem fear christmas time,
Dey wanna enjoy it, dey say humans
    destroyed it
An humans are out of dere mind,
Yeah, I got lots of friends who
    are turkeys
Dey all hav a right to a life,
15 Not to be caged up an genetically
    made up
By any farmer an his wife.

Turkeys just wanna play reggae
Turkeys just wanna hip-hop
Can yu imagine a nice young
    turkey saying,
20 'I cannot wait for de chop',
Turkeys like getting presents,
    dey wanna watch christmas TV,
Turkeys hav brains an turkeys
    feel pain
In many ways like yu an me.

I once knew a turkey called …
    Turkey
25 He said 'Benji explain to me please,
Who put de turkey in christmas
An what happens to christmas
    trees?',
I said 'I am not too sure turkey
But it's nothing to do wid
    Christ Mass
30 Humans get greedy an waste more
    dan need be
An business men mek loadsa cash'.

Be nice to yu turkey dis christmas
Invite dem indoors fe sum greens
Let dem eat cake an let dem partake
35 In a plate of organic grown beans,
Be nice to yu turkey dis christmas
An spare dem de cut of de knife,
Join Turkeys United an dey'll be
    delighted
An yu will mek new friends
    'FOR LIFE'.

Benjamin Zephaniah

4 Answer the following questions about the poem.

    a Stanza 1 begins 'Be nice ...'. Why does the writer feel we should be nice to turkeys at Christmas? List his reasons.

    b What sub-heading could be given to Stanza 1?

    c Which one or two lines do you feel best sum up Stanza 2? Why?

    d In Stanza 3, why does the turkey call the poet 'Benji'?

    e What explanation does the writer give to the turkey in Stanza 3 about why turkeys are killed at Christmas?

    f In Stanza 4, why do you think the writer chose to end his poem with the two words 'FOR LIFE'?

    g Why do you think the poet wrote these final words in upper case?

Using supporting evidence to back up your ideas

When you express an opinion about the meaning of a poem, it is important to use evidence from the poem to support your point of view. Here is a statement that could be supported with evidence from the poem.

The poet's idea	The supporting evidence
The poet feels it is wrong to kill turkeys at Christmas.	'Turkeys hav brains an turkeys feel pain'

Activity 13

1 Find other ideas or feelings that are expressed in the poem and provide evidence to support them.

2 Swap your list of ideas and supporting evidence with a partner. Use a scale like this one to assess their work.

* * *	* *	*
Has found lots of different ideas in the poem and all are supported with evidence.	Has found some ideas but has missed a few others. Most are supported with evidence.	Has found one or two ideas but the supporting evidence is not very well chosen.

If you decide your partner should get only one *, show them another few ideas they could have found in the poem and explain which parts of the poem provide the evidence for that point.

Assessment task

DRAGONFLIES

You are going to compare the poem 'Dragonflies' with an extract from 'The Two Voices'. One of the poems was written quite recently and the other was written more than a hundred years ago. You will be thinking about the ways in which poets use techniques to make these insects seem special.

Read the poems below and answer the questions that follow on page 80.

Dragonflies

They used to fly
over all the ponds
in summer, Granny says

like sparkling sapphire helicopters,
5   purple aeroplanes,
with eyes of bright **topaz**,
wings flashing emerald light,
brightening the countryside
in their jewelled flight.

10   Sun-glow brilliance winging
over every pond,
someday I hope to see one
– smallest last dragon.

Joan Poulson

> **Word bank**
>
> **topaz** a kind of jewel

from The Two Voices

Today I saw the dragon-fly
Come from the wells where he did lie.
An inner impulse rent the **veil**
Of his old husk: from head to tail
5   Came out clear plates of sapphire **mail**.
He dried his wings: like **gauze** they grew;
Through crofts and pastures wet with dew
A living flash of light, he flew.

Alfred, Lord Tennyson

> **Word bank**
>
> **an inner impulse** a force inside
> **rent** tore
> **veil** a covering for the head
> **mail** armour
> **gauze** a thin, see-through kind of cloth

1 a How does the writer of 'Dragonflies' use comparisons to make dragonflies seem very 'special' things? Look, in particular, at the second stanza.

 b What comparisons does the writer of 'The Two Voices' use to describe a dragonfly

2 Copy and complete the table below so that you can list the similarities and differences between the poems. Think about the following things and jot down your ideas in the table.

	'Dragonflies'	**'The Two Voices'**
Each writer's feelings about dragonflies and reason for writing about them	My ideas:	My ideas:
	My evidence:	My evidence:
The methods used by each writer to describe the dragonfly. Think about similes, metaphors and rhyme.	My ideas:	My ideas:
	My evidence:	My evidence:
The ways the poems are organised. Think about how the writers have arranged their poems into stanzas.	My ideas:	My ideas:
	My evidence:	My evidence:

3 Which poem is more modern? Prepare a list of clues that helped you reach your conclusion.

4 Which poem do you prefer? Why?

4 Capture the moment

The bigger picture

In this unit you will explore how writers use words to capture a moment or important event in their lives. At the end of the unit you will write a lively and interesting account of a moment or incident in your life.

WHAT? You will:
- explore surface meaning and hidden meaning
- develop your skills in choosing the best words and sentence structures
- revise how to use the first person and the past and present tenses

HOW? by:
- closely reading three texts, thinking about meanings and making deductions based on what you have read
- examining the effects of words and sentence structure
- practising writing in the first person and using the past and present tenses

WHY? because:
- close reading helps you to work out what writers are really saying
- to be a good writer you need to use a wide range of words and sentence structures to interest your reader
- you need to be able to control tenses in order to control your ideas and make sense for your reader

Remembering recount texts

You may have studied recount texts before. Here are some of their
main features.

- Their purpose is to retell events.
- They are usually written in the past tense.
- They are often organised in chronological order (the order in which
  things happened).
- They often use words or phrases that signal time, for example: *then*, *later*,
  from that moment. You may know these as connectives.

Activity 1

The following extract is from an autobiography. It tells us about an incident in
the author's childhood. As you read it, work out how many features of recount
texts it has.

> Not long after Father and Niang returned from Tianjin, Mr and Mrs Huang came
> to visit. They brought gifts for all seven of us children in a large cardboard box
> with several holes punched in the lid. Before her marriage, Mrs Huang had
> worked for a few years at Grand Aunt's bank, sharing a booth with Aunt Baba
> 5 and our real mama. The Huangs therefore knew of Father's first marriage and
> the existence of all seven children.
>
> When we opened the gift box from the Huangs, we were delighted to find
> seven little baby ducklings. As usual, Fourth Brother picked first, followed by
> Little Sister, Big Sister, Big Brother, Second Brother and Third Brother. By the
> 10 time my turn arrived, I was left with the tiniest, scrawniest baby bird. I picked
> her up, cupped her in my hand and carried her **gingerly** into my room. The little
> duckling cocked her head to one side and looked at me with dark dewy round
> eyes. She waddled unsteadily and pecked the floor, looking for worms and
> seeds. She seemed so helpless with her soft yellow feathers, slender twiggy
> 15 legs and small webbed feet. One **gust** of wind and
> she would be blown away. I felt very protective.
>
> From that moment, I took the duckling to
> my heart. For the first time, I had a pet of
> my very own. At school, I proudly
> 20 described my duckling to my classmates.
> As I spoke, I felt a warm, tender glow
> spreading all through me. I named my
> duckling Precious Little Treasure (Xiao
> Bao-bei). Wu Chun-mei advised me to
> 25 call it PLT for short. I couldn't wait to rush
> home from school, carry PLT to my room,
> bathe and feed her, and do my homework
> with PLT wandering between the beds and my
> desk. It comforted me to know I was needed.

Word bank

gingerly in a
careful or cautious
way
gust a brief, strong
rush of wind

From *Chinese Cinderella* by Adeline Yen Mah

Retelling a story

To show your understanding of this text, you are going to explain what it is about to a partner. To do this well you need to focus on the main points of the story. They are listed below but they are not in order.

Activity 2

1 Put the main points in the correct chronological order. Make a table like the one below to help you.

g								

a The narrator got the smallest bird.

b The Huangs knew about all seven children.

c The narrator described the duckling to her classmates.

d The Huangs brought several ducklings as presents for the children.

e The narrator nicknamed the duckling 'PLT'.

f The narrator felt very protective towards the duckling.

g Mr and Mrs Huang visited the narrator's family.

h The narrator named the duckling 'Precious Little Treasure'.

 Sharpen punctuation

Capital letters

Capital letters are used for the names of people and places. List as many different examples in the extract on page 82 as you can where capital letters are used for names.

1 Why do you think the writer uses capital letters when she refers to her brothers and sisters?

2 Explain why the writer uses the capitals 'PLT'.

2 Using your own words, explain what the extract on page 82 is about. Aim to make your explanation accurate and clear.

 Feedback

1 Assess your partner's work. Use the following questions as a guide for assessment and award a mark of 1 (needs a bit more work), 2 (good) or 3 (excellent or very good).
   • Did they include all the main points?
   • Did they sequence the details in the correct order?
   • Did they make the account clear?

2 Explain the marks you have given your partner.

3 Ask your partner to explain the marks they have given you.

4 Record the marks your partner gave you and write down two ways in which you could improve your explanation.

Interpreting details

In the extract from *Chinese Cinderella* the writer leaves several clues that tell the reader more about the lives of the people in this family. Copy and complete the table below, saying what you think the clues in the first column really mean.

What the writer says	What this makes me think
The Huangs therefore knew of Father's first marriage and the existence of all seven children. (lines 5–6)	It suggests that most people didn't know about the first marriage and all seven children.
As usual, Fourth Brother picked first, followed by Little Sister, Big Sister, Big Brother, Second Brother and Third Brother. (lines 8–9)	This makes me think that …
It comforted me to know I was needed. (line 29)	

Thinking about tense

Recount texts are often written in the past tense because they are about things that happened some time ago. There are two main forms of the past tense.

Simple past:
I walked
We thought

Continuous past:
I was walking
We were thinking

We use the simple past mainly to describe completed actions. We use the continuous past to describe actions that go on for a period of time.

Activity 3

1 In the extract from *Chinese Cinderella* on page 82, the writer mostly uses the simple past. Copy the following lines and underline the writer's use of simple past.

> I picked her up, cupped her in my hand and carried her gingerly into my room. The little duckling cocked her head to one side and looked at me with dark dewy round eyes. She waddled unsteadily and pecked the floor, looking for worms and seeds. (lines 10–14)

Sharpen spelling

Simple past tense

- When writing the simple past tense you usually add the suffix -*ed*:
  pick ⟶ pick<u>ed</u>   look ⟶ look<u>ed</u>
- Sometimes you need to double the consonant and add -*ed*:
  cup ⟶ cupped
- If the verb already ends in *e* just add *d*:
  waddle ⟶ waddle<u>d</u>
- If the verb ends in -*y* after a consonant, you need to change the *y* to *i* and add -*ed*:
  carry ⟶ carr<u>ied</u>
- Some verbs have irregular past tenses:
  feel ⟶ <u>felt</u>   take ⟶ <u>took</u>

Find and list other examples of the simple past tense in the extract on page 82. Identify which group from above they belong to. Which group contains the most words? This is the most common form of the simple past tense.

2 Write a paragraph recounting what you did this morning before you came to school. Aim to use both the simple and the continuous forms of the past tense. Highlight every time you use the past tense. Identify whether it is simple past or continuous past.

Making predictions

As we read, we often predict what will happen next. Our predictions are based on our experiences and on clues given by the writer.

 Activity 4

1 Remind yourself of what happened in the extract from *Chinese Cinderella* on page 82.
Then write down:
a what you think will happen next
b the clues that make you think this.

2 Now read the extract that follows and check your prediction to see how close you were.

Highlight thinking

Making predictions
When making predictions you need to draw on your knowledge and experiences.

In doing this it can help to group (or classify) information. You can take the whole picture and break it down into key areas. For this story it could be what you know about: the girl, the duckling, their relationship, the girl's position in the family. Given what you know, what do you think is most likely to happen?

Think about where else you might use these skills.

Adeline dotes on PLT, even risking the vicious bite of Jackie, the family's German Shepherd dog, to dig up worms for her. The story continues one evening after the family meal.

'Since it's so hot tonight,' Father suggested, 'why don't we cool off in the garden after dinner? It will also give us a chance to test Jackie's obedience.' He turned to Big Brother. 'Go fetch one of those ducklings that the Huangs brought. We'll have some fun tonight!'

5   There was a momentary silence. To us children, Father's announcement was like a death sentence. Immediately, I had a picture in my mind of my pet being torn to pieces between Jackie's frothing, ravenous jaws. I held myself rigid, in a world full of dread, knowing with absolute certainty that the doomed duckling would be mine.

10   Big Brother scraped back his chair, ran upstairs and came down with PLT. Everyone avoided looking at me. Father strode into the garden with PLT on his palm and sat down on a lounge chair. We children sprawled in a semi-circle on the grass. Jackie greeted his master joyfully, wagging his tail and jumping up and down with happiness.

15   Father released PLT and placed her in the centre of the lawn. My little pet appeared bewildered by all the commotion. She stood quite still for a few moments, trying to get her bearings: a small, yellow, defenceless creature beset with perils. I sat stiffly with downcast eyes. For a moment, I was unable

Word bank

riveted firmly fixed
palpable able to be touched
irrevocably cannot be changed

20 to focus properly. 'Don't move, PLT! Please don't move!' I prayed silently. 'As long as you keep still, you have a chance!'

Jackie was ordered to 'sit' about two metres away. He sat on his hind legs with his large tongue hanging out, panting away. His fierce eyes were **riveted** on his prey. Father kept two fingers on his collar while Jackie fidgeted and strained restlessly.

25 The tension seemed **palpable** while I hoped against hope that fate could be side-stepped in some way. Then PLT cocked her head in that achingly familiar way of hers and spotted me. Chirping happily, she waddled unsteadily towards me. Tempted beyond endurance, Jackie sprang forward. In one powerful leap, he broke away from Father's restraint and pounced on PLT, who looked up at 30 me pleadingly, as if I was supposed to have an answer to all her terror.

Father dashed over, enraged by Jackie's defiance. Immediately, Jackie released the bird from his jaws, but with a pang I saw PLT's left leg dangling lifelessly and her tiny, 35 webbed foot twisted at a grotesque angle. Blood spurted briskly from an open wound.

I was overwhelmed with horror. My whole world turned desolate. I ran over without a word, cradled PLT tenderly in my arms and 40 carried her upstairs. Placing her on my bed, I wrapped my mortally wounded pet in my best school scarf and lay down next to her. It was a night of grief I have never forgotten.

I lay there with my eyes closed pretending 45 to be asleep but was actually hopelessly awake. Surely everything would remain the same as long as I kept my eyes shut and did not look at PLT. Perhaps, when I finally opened them again after wishing very hard 50 all night, PLT's leg would miraculously be healed.

In spite of everything, I must have dozed off because at the break of dawn, I woke up with a jerk. Beside me, PLT was now completely 55 still. The horrors of the previous evening flooded back and everything was as bad as before. Worse, because PLT was now **irrevocably** dead. Gone forever.

From *Chinese Cinderella* by Adeline Yen Mah

Responding to the story

To be a skilled reader, you need to be able to explain your thoughts and feelings about what you have read. The following activities will help you with this.

Activity 5

1 Remind yourself of both extracts from *Chinese Cinderella* (pages 82 and 85–6). Then note your answers to questions a–f.

   a   Do you have a pet? Could you identify with the writer's feelings for her pet?

   b   What do you think of Father's actions?

   c   What do you think of Big Brother's actions?

   d   How does the writer show the vulnerability of the duckling in lines 15–18?

   e   How does the writer create a sense of tension in lines 15–24?

   f   How does the writer show her pain in lines 37–42?

2 Write down any other important questions that should be asked. Explain why you think these questions are important.

3 Use your notes to help you write a paragraph explaining your thoughts and feelings about the story. You could begin like this:

When I started to read the story I ...

Using short sentences for effect

Writers use short sentences for different reasons. They may use them to:

- emphasise a particular point
- create tension
- speed up the pace for greater effect

- convey thought or speech
- show strong emotion
- slow the pace down for greater effect.

The writer of *Chinese Cinderella* uses several short, simple sentences for effect. A simple sentence consists of one clause which usually contains a subject and a verb:

subject verb

He turned to Big Brother. (line 3)

Activity 6

1 Look at the whole extract on pages 85–6. Find and list the short, simple sentences the writer has used. For each one, identify the subject and the verb.

2 From your list, highlight *four* sentences that you think work well. For each one, explain why you think the writer has used it.

Focusing on verbs and adverbs

Writers choose verbs and adverbs very carefully to suggest certain things.

Verbs

- A verb is a word that expresses an action, a happening, a process or a state. It is sometimes called a 'doing' or 'being' word.
- In the example below the verbs are highlighted.

  Big Brother <u>scraped</u> back his chair, <u>ran</u> upstairs and came down with PLT. (line 10)

Adverbs

- An adverb is a word that gives extra meaning to a verb.
- In the example below the adverbs are highlighted.

  Chirping <u>happily</u>, she waddled <u>unsteadily</u> towards me. (lines 27–8)

  'Happily' tells us how she was chirping and 'unsteadily' tells us how she waddled.

Activity 7

1 Copy and complete the following table by:
   a highlighting all the verbs and adverbs
   b saying what extra things you learn from the adverbs.

Answer the questions in the table to help you think about the effects of the adverbs.

Examples of verbs and adverbs	The effects of the adverbs
Jackie greeted his master joyfully. (line 13)	What does the adverb tell you about the dog's feelings for his master?
I sat stiffly with downcast eyes. (line 18)	What does the adverb tell you about the narrator's feelings as she sat?
Blood spurted briskly from an open wound. (line 36)	What does the adverb suggest about the seriousness of the wound?
I ... cradled PLT tenderly in my arms. (lines 38–9)	What does the adverb tell you about the narrator's feelings for PLT?

2 Write two sentences to describe each of the following. Choose your verbs and adverbs carefully to create the best effect, and underline them.
   a An old man walking down a street.
   b A child learning to ride a bike.
   c A footballer about to take a penalty.

Here is an example.

The toddler <u>steered</u> the bike <u>recklessly</u> on to the road. He almost <u>collided</u> with a parked car, then <u>stopped</u> <u>abruptly</u> and <u>cried</u>.

 Sharpen spelling

Adverbs

Adverbs often end in *-ly*, for example: *joyfully, stiffly, silently, happily, unsteadily*.

When adding *-ly* you do not usually change the spelling of the root word unless it ends in *-y*.

Work out what to do when the root word ends in *-y*. Write a rule for adding *-ly* to words ending in *-y*.

✓ **Progress check**

Look back at the learning you have done so far in this unit. You have:
- revised the features of recount texts
- thought about how capital letters are used for names
- retold a story using the main details
- interpreted the details of a story
- thought about how to use the past tense
- thought about how to spell words in the past tense
- made a prediction
- expressed your thoughts and feelings
- considered how short sentences are used for effect
- focused on using verbs and adverbs for effect.

1 Which two things on this list do you feel you have done best?
Write them down and draw a star by them.

2 Which two things do you think you need to learn more about?
Write them down and draw an arrow beside them. For each one,
write a sentence explaining why you feel unsure about it.

Planning to write

You are going to write about a time in your past when you were either very
happy or very sad.

 Activity 8

1 To help you recall the time, talk with a partner about the answers to the
questions below. Record your answers briefly on a spidergram.

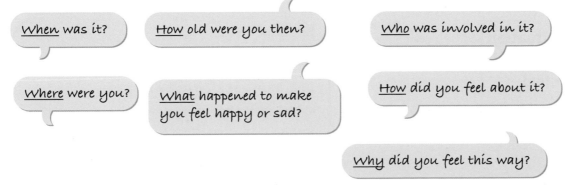

When was it?   How old were you then?   Who was involved in it?

Where were you?   What happened to make you feel happy or sad?   How did you feel about it?

Why did you feel this way?

Notice how answering the questions: When? How? Where? Who? What? and
Why? helps you to gather your ideas together.

2 Use the flow diagram below to help you organise your ideas. Use notes rather than full sentences. At the side are some useful reminders about recount texts to help you.

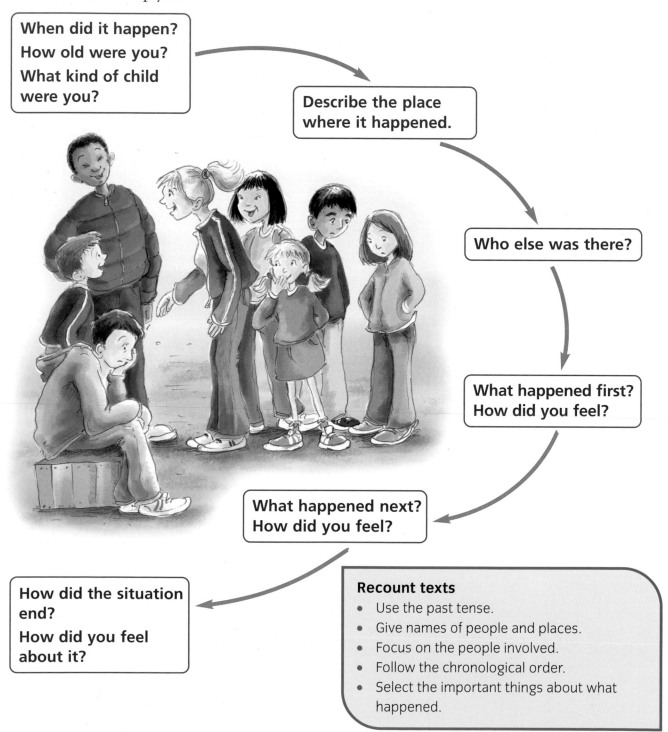

When did it happen?
How old were you?
What kind of child were you?

Describe the place where it happened.

Who else was there?

What happened first?
How did you feel?

What happened next?
How did you feel?

How did the situation end?
How did you feel about it?

Recount texts
- Use the past tense.
- Give names of people and places.
- Focus on the people involved.
- Follow the chronological order.
- Select the important things about what happened.

Keep your flow diagram. You will need it for the assessment task at the end of the unit (see pages 105–06).

 **Feedback**

Your flow diagram plan should show:
- what you are going to write about
- the order in which you are going to write.

Once you have finished your plan you should be able to start writing.

1 Assess how well your plan would help you to write. Copy and shade this diagram to show how successful you think your plan is.

H O W	G O O D	M Y	P L A N	I S

unhelpful   **quite helpful**   **very helpful**   **brilliant**

2 Compare your plan with a partner's and note the differences between them. Think about how you could improve your plan, perhaps by adding detail. Make the improvements before moving on.

Reading meaning in pictures

Sometimes people combine writing and drawing skills to recount a story in cartoon format. An example of this is *Ethel and Ernest*. This is a story written and illustrated by Raymond Briggs about his parents. Study the first three frames on page 92 and then answer the questions below.

Activity 9

1 a Who do you think has passed the scholarship?
   b How does the woman feel about this? How do you know this?
   c Who do you think the man is?
   d What do the man's clothes tell you about him?
   e What do you think the man is worried about?
   f Why are different types of print used?
   g Why are the speech bubbles drawn differently?

2 Carefully read the rest of the story on pages 92–4 (frames 4–12).
For each frame say:
- what you find out from the words
- what you find out from the pictures.

3 Discuss your answers with a partner. Talk about:
- the similarities and differences between your answers
- the way the words link/don't link with the pictures.

Making deductions

When we read closely we make deductions based on the details we are given in the text.

Activity 10

Now you have read the whole text on pages 92–4, consider the list of statements below. Copy and complete the table to show whether you agree or disagree with each statement and give a reason. The first one has been done for you.

a The mother is protective of her son.
b The father is happy that his son is going to grammar school.
c The boy's uniform is expensive.
d The mother doesn't like to boast.
e The father is more sensitive than the mother.
f The mother panics when things go wrong.
g The son is ashamed of what he has done.
h The mother always tells the truth.

 Sharpen punctuation

Apostrophes

When people speak they sometimes shorten two words into one. For example, *it is* becomes *it's*. An apostrophe is put in the place of the missing letter(s):

it is → it's

1 Copy out the following and shorten each into one word using apostrophes. Highlight the letter(s) you have dropped and the apostrophe.

- he is
- they are
- should not
- did not
- whatever is
- he has
- can not
- do not

2 Think of another six examples of words that could be shortened by using an apostrophe. Test a partner by asking them to write the shortened form.

Statement	Agree/disagree	Reason
a The mother is protective of her son.	Agree	She tells him to keep away from the milk van saying it's dangerous.
b The father is happy that his son is going to grammar school.		

Thinking about tense

Different tenses are used to describe things that happen at different times. It's possible to use different tenses in the same sentence or speech.

simple past ———
present ———
continuous
future ———

Your son (was apprehended) breaking and entering the Golf Club and stealing valuable billiard cues. (He's) lucky. THIS TIME (we are letting) him off with a caution. Next time (it will be) BORSTAL.

——— simple present

95

Activity 11

Using speech bubbles write a conversation that could have taken place between the policeman and the boy's father. In it the policeman warns the father about the boy's friends and the father offers to pay for the damage done at the golf club. Identify the different tenses you use.

Making pictures with words

As you can see, the pictures on pages 92–4 give the reader information that the writer would otherwise have to give us in words.

Activity 12

1 Look at frame 10 on page 94, after the mother discovers her son has been stealing. If there were no pictures the writer would need to describe the scene in words. The description might read like this:

The mother was very angry. She raised her hands in the air and clenched her fists. She looked as though she was going to hit her son. She shouted at him loudly, 'You wicked, wicked boy! I could kill you!' The boy said nothing. He stood with his back to his mother and hung his head in shame.

2 Now look at frame 11 opposite. Tell the story of this frame. You can either tell it to a partner or write it down. Remember to describe:
   • the scene
   • what is happening
   • what is said
   • the way it is said.

Sharpen punctuation

Exclamation marks
An exclamation mark can be used:
   • at the end of a sentence, for example, *'He's passed the scholarship!'*
   • after an interjection, for example, *'Ooooh!'*

Exclamation marks are used to show strong emotion such as delight, anger or horror.

1 Write down examples of the use of exclamation marks in the frames on pages 92–4. You should find at least eight.
2 For each one identify the emotion that the exclamation mark shows.

Extending your vocabulary

We can capture the way something is said by using a range of different verbs.
Instead of 'he said' we can write 'he …'

asked **answered** *claimed* *shouted* **replied**

muttered **screamed** laughed *giggled* BEGGED

stated exclaimed enquired **taunted** roared

Activity 13

1 Above are just *some* of the verbs we can use instead of 'said'. Write a list of at least ten others. You could use a thesaurus to help you.

2 Rewrite what is said in frames 1–7 on pages 92–3. Use speech marks around the spoken words and different verbs to describe how the words are said. The first four have been done for you.

'He's passed the scholarship!' she cried.

'I hope he won't get too posh for us,' he muttered.

'There, madam,' he declared.

'He's going to the grammar school!' she exclaimed.

Feedback

1 With a partner look at the verbs you chose in Activity 13, question 2 to describe the way the words are spoken. Say the words aloud, using the verbs as a guide to how they should be said.

2 Compare your choices with your partner. Are you happy with your choices? If you are, tick the verbs you have chosen. If you aren't, think again and change them.

Matching pictures and words

Look back at the flow diagram you completed in Activity 8 on page 90, about a time when you felt happy or sad. In the fourth box you described what happened first and how you felt.

Activity 14
Produce one or two cartoon frames to represent what you described in the fourth box. Remember to:
a use spoken words only
b give enough detail in the pictures to help get across what is happening and how people are feeling.

Progress check

Here is another frame from later in the same story. Look at it, then check your progress by answering the questions that follow.

1 a What is the mother feeling?
   b How does the picture show you this?

2 a What different types of print are used?
   b Why are the different types of print used?

3 Use three different verbs to show how the mother says the words: 'He's passed! He's passed the school certificate!' she
_____ .

4 Explain why, in the sentence 'He's passed!', there is:
a an apostrophe
b an exclamation mark.

If you have been able to do all four activities in this progress check you are ready to move on. If not, look back over pages 91–8.

Investigating clues

Writers often give the reader clues to help them work out different things. In his book *The Crocodile Hunter*, Steve Irwin recounts how, with the help of his dog Chilli, he finally managed to capture a legendary crocodile and save him from dangerous hunters. As you read, answer the questions.

To catch a croc …

1 List the clues in the first paragraph that tell you:
- where the story is set
- that the writer has been trying to catch the crocodile for some time.

Chilli and I had become part of the **mangroves**; birds and wallabies accepted us as part of their everyday life. My stalking skills became very refined. Sometimes I'd squat for hours in the insect-infested mangroves, camouflaged with leaves and mud, just hoping to glimpse my target crocodile. But nothing,
5 not one thing. I was starting to lose the plot – I calculated that it was over eighteen months since I'd first anticipated catching this elusive old croc.

2 In lines 7–24 below, the writer uses connectives that signal time as a way of organising his ideas. The first connective is: 'Then at the cracka one morning …' (line 7)

The last connective is: 'It was different on the river this morning.' (line 24)

Find and list the other five connectives. Use all seven connectives to work out how many days are covered in this passage.

Then at the **cracka** one morning I was doing my routine trap run when I noticed a lead-in bait had gone. Excitedly I jammed the boat into the mangroves and grabbed the bait's nylon cord. It had been pulled so hard it had been flung up
10 into the branches, severed by a large downward force. The entire fist-sized piece of fresh pork and part of the nylon cord were gone. Was this the croc's second mistake? I was so excited I didn't even swat the ants biting my eyelids. It was the trap I'd anticipated he'd hit, my biggest trap in the wildlife 'hot spot'.

You beauty!
15 That day Chilli and I got a fairly large putrid piece of meat to use in re-baiting the trap. I parked my boat way downstream and carried the bait in over my shoulder. This way I would leave no tracks or boat disturbance around the entrance to the trap. Surely the rotting meat would be enticing to him.

That night I couldn't sleep. It took forever for the sun to appear. First light I
20 raced straight to the trap. Nothing. Nothing touched, no signs, no slides, no marks – nothing.

The next night came around; it was a struggle to sleep.

At first light Chilli and I casually fueled up and headed for the traps. It was different on the river this morning.

Word bank

mangroves tropical evergreen trees
cracka Australian slang meaning 'crack of dawn' or 'daybreak'

3 Predict what will happen next. Give two reasons, based on what you have read so far that make you think this. When you have read the rest of the story, check your prediction to see how close you were.

4 In lines 25–38 that follow, the writer uses both the past and the present tenses. Identify where he uses the present tense. Suggest two reasons for using the present tense.

25 As I rounded the bend and zoomed into the 'hot spot' trap, I got the shock of my life. Adrenaline surged through my swollen veins. 'This is it, Chilli! This is it! Stay cool, Steve.'

30 The mangroves erupted; a huge jolting force pounded the bow of the boat. Panic was pushing my eyeballs out – I must stay in control! Oh crikey! His tail and back leg are out of the trap – my trap's not big enough! The tide's coming and already he's surrounded by water. Think quick! Keep a grip … get a top-jaw rope.

35 Securing the boat in the trap entrance, I climbed into the mangroves with a couple of top-jaw ropes and headed in toward the croc's head. *Whack!* As soon as he saw me he head-butted a huge mangrove tree and snapped it off.

'Settle, boy, settle!'

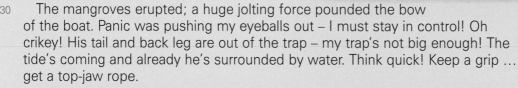

5 Just like the extracts from *Chinese Cinderella*, the events in Steve Irwin's story are recounted in chronological order. Think about why chronological order might be a useful way of organising ideas in lines 25–38.

Whack! He clobbered another huge tree. Once around the front of his head, I
40 snapped off a stick and tried to thread a top-jaw rope between his massive yellow teeth. He lunged straight at me, ripping the stick and rope clean out of my hands. He snorted and blew mucus and spray into my face. His eyes were wide, full of anger and fear.

45 *Whoosh!* The croc exploded in a thrashing frenzy. He gripped the trap in his teeth and went into a series of violent death rolls. The instant he stopped I positioned my top-jaw rope stick, then jammed it between those huge teeth and pushed it out the other side. Scampering between the aerial mangrove roots, I seized the rope end before he had time to react. I sensed he was tired.

Finally I secured my first top-jaw rope and hastily knotted it to the nearest
50 tree. I readied another rope. As soon as I was in range to secure it he exploded again. He struck out at me with a bone-crunching head thrash, then spun into another death roll. This time the jaw rope wrapped around his head, and the tree it was tied to was winched down until it snapped off. He settled and I regained the rope and secured it to the biggest tree in the vicinity. Hoping it
55 would hold, I secured another two top-jaw ropes while he recovered.

Now that he was restrained, I had to shift him. Happy that he was temporarily secured, I sped back to my camp.

From *The Crocodile Hunter* by Steve and Terri Irwin

6 The writer describes in detail how he caught the crocodile. He could just have written: 'The crocodile fought back but I defeated him.' Suggest at least two reasons why the writer gives the reader this detail.

7 a How does the start of the last paragraph show us that the recount is coming to an end?
  b How does the last sentence signal that:
   • this part of the recount is ended
   • there is more to come?

 Sharpen punctuation

Hyphens
Look at these examples of how hyphens are used throughout the extracts.
• insect-infested mangroves
• fist-sized piece
• bone-crunching head thrash
• lead-in bait
• top-jaw rope

1 Identify, by line number, where each example appears in the extract.
2 Work out what the hyphens have in common.
3 Explain why the hyphen is used. Write down one rule for when you should use hyphens.

Examining a writer's techniques

Writers use a range of techniques to make their writing more interesting for the reader.

Carefully re-read the following lines from *The Crocodile Hunter* and the information on the writer's techniques.

Technique 1
The writer uses onomatopoeia with words that sound like the sound of the action being described. He does this, almost like sound effects in a film, to make it seem more real.

Technique 2
The writer uses verbs of action. These are verbs that help to create a sense of action and excitement.

> *Whack!* He clobbered another huge tree. Once around the front of his head, I snapped off a stick and tried to thread a top-jaw rope between his massive yellow teeth. He lunged straight at me, ripping the stick and rope clean out of my hands. He snorted and blew mucus and spray into my face. His eyes were wide, full of anger and fear.
>
> *Whoosh!* The croc exploded in a thrashing frenzy. He gripped the trap in his teeth and went into a series of violent death rolls. The instant he stopped I positioned my top-jaw rope stick, then jammed it between those huge teeth and pushed it out the other side. Scampering between the aerial mangrove roots, I seized the rope end before he had time to react. I sensed he was tired.

Technique 3
The writer uses a range of sentence structures.

- He uses **simple sentences** which communicate one idea at a time and make complete sense:
  'He clobbered another huge tree'.

- He uses **compound sentences** which link two or more simple sentences with a conjunction such as *and*, or and *but*:
  'He snorted and blew mucus and spray into my face.'
  He snorted. + (He) blew mucus and spray into my face.

- He uses **complex sentences** which communicate more than one idea by using clauses. The clauses are sometimes separated by a comma:

main clause   subordinate clause

'He lunged straight at me, ripping the stick and rope clean out of my hands.'

This sentence has a main clause, which is complete on its own and can form a complete sentence. It also has a subordinate clause, which cannot exist on its own.

Activity 15

1 Think about Technique 1. Make a list of any other onomatopoeic words you can think of.

2 Think about Technique 2. Write out the verbs of action in the order in which they appear in the extract on page 102.

- Write a **C** beside those that show the actions of the crocodile.
- Write an **S** beside those that show the actions of the writer, Steve Irwin.

What do you notice about these verbs?

Activity 16

1 Look again at the extract from *The Crocodile Hunter* on pages 99–101. Make sure you understand Technique 3 and the difference between the three sentence types by copying one example of:

a a simple sentence (identify its subject and verb)

b a compound sentence (show which two simple sentences are linked)

c a complex sentence (identify its main clause and its subordinate clause).

2 The paragraph below is clear but boring. It is written in simple sentences. In pairs or on your own, re-write it in a more detailed and interesting way. In your re-write make sure you use:

a onomatopoeia

b verbs of action

c simple, compound and complex sentences.

> The dog ran across the park. A boy ran after it. The boy shouted at the dog to stop. The dog kept running. The dog ran in front of a jogger. The jogger fell over. Then the dog saw a duck. It was walking by the side of the lake. The dog barked loudly. The duck ran to the water. The dog almost caught it. The duck got into the water just in time.

You could start like this:

Having slipped its lead, the crafty dog raced across the park while the boy chased it helplessly.

Feedback

1 In your re-write, highlight or underline and label an example of:
   a onomatopoeia
   b a verb of action
   c a simple sentence
   d a compound sentence
   e a complex sentence.

2 In small groups read the re-writes of two or three other individuals or pairs. Decide which re-write is the best. Give two or three reasons for your decision.

Using the first person

Look back at the extracts from *Chinese Cinderella* (pages 82 and 85–6) and *The Crocodile Hunter* (pages 99–101). In both texts the writers are recounting something that has happened to them. They both write in the first person, using *I* for singular and *we* for plural.

Activity 17

1 Talk with a partner about the advantages and disadvantages of writing in the first person. Below are some statements. Decide if:
   a you agree with these statements
   b the things mentioned are advantages or disadvantages.

Writing in the first person:
- lets the reader get inside the mind of the writer
- makes it seem real because the writers are describing their own lives
- lets the writer stand back and judge things without emotion
- gives only one point of view
- makes the writing more personal
- helps the reader to see the writer from other people's point of view
- helps the reader to understand the writer.

2 Copy the table below and complete it by recording your decisions.

Writing in the first person	
Advantages	**Disadvantages**

◒ Assessment task

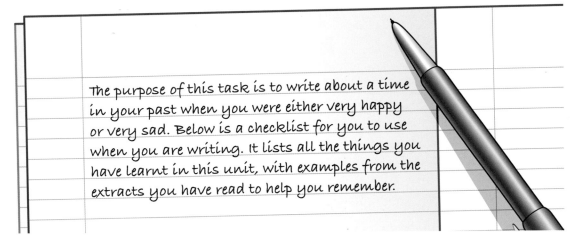

The purpose of this task is to write about a time in your past when you were either very happy or very sad. Below is a checklist for you to use when you are writing. It lists all the things you have learnt in this unit, with examples from the extracts you have read to help you remember.

Step 1
Remind yourself of the things you need to do when writing a recount text.

- Set the scene.

  Chilli and I had become part of the mangroves; birds and wallabies accepted us as part of their everyday life. (lines 1–2, *The Crocodile Hunter*)

- Use a range of verbs and adverbs.

  Chirping happily, she waddled unsteadily towards me. (lines 27–8, *Chinese Cinderella*)

- Create pictures with words.

- Use a range of punctuation to make your meaning clear.

  'He's passed the scholarship!'
  (frame 1, page 92, *Ethel and Ernest*)

- Recount events in chronological order using connectives that signal time.

  From that moment, I took the duckling to my heart. (lines 17–18, *Chinese Cinderella*)

- Write in the past tense most of the time.

> I picked her up, cupped her in my hand and carried her gingerly into my room. (lines 10–11, *Chinese Cinderella*)

- Use a range of sentence structures.

> His eyes were wide, full of anger and fear. *Whoosh!* The croc exploded in a thrashing frenzy. He gripped the trap in his teeth and went into a series of violent death rolls. (lines 42–5, *The Crocodile Hunter*)

Step 2

Turn to the flow diagram you made on page 90. You may have better ideas for writing now than when you first made your plan. Here are some possible subjects you may not have thought of:

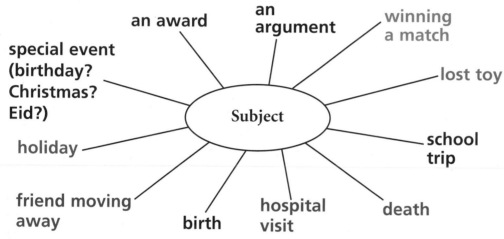

an award · an argument · winning a match · special event (birthday? Christmas? Eid?) · lost toy · holiday · **Subject** · school trip · friend moving away · birth · hospital visit · death

Spend ten minutes reviewing your plan. Make changes or add to it.

Step 3

Write your recount.
- Aim to write 300–500 words.
- Remember to write in paragraphs.
- Stop often to re-read what you have written to check you are expressing your ideas clearly.

Step 4

Check what you have written. Imagine you are reading it aloud to the class. Ask yourself these questions.
a Does my writing make sense?
b Is it interesting?
c Have I given enough detail?

Use your answers to these questions to help you improve your writing.

5 Top tips

The bigger picture

In this unit you will investigate how writers influence, persuade and advise their readers. At the end of the unit you will study a text to work out the techniques the writer has used to get the readers' attention and to give them advice.

WHAT? You will:
- explore different types of advice
- develop your skills in matching tone to purpose and audience
- extend your range of sentence structures
- revise the use of modal verbs and imperatives

HOW? by:
- closely reading different types of advice and examining the way writers influence their readers
- examining the presentational features used in different types of text
- practising writing different kinds of advice

WHY? because:
- reading closely helps you to work out how writers create advice texts
- to be a good writer you need to adapt your vocabulary and sentence structure to purpose and audience
- you need to use presentational features effectively to attract and keep your readers' attention

What is advice?

Advice is something we give and receive in many different ways.

Activity 1

1 To help you decide exactly what advice is, talk with a partner about the following statements. Place them in order of importance, putting the one you most agree with first and the one you least agree with last.

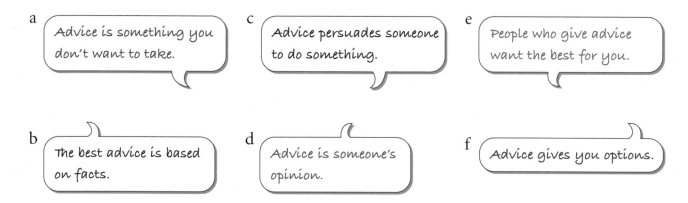

a *Advice is something you don't want to take.*

c *Advice persuades someone to do something.*

e *People who give advice want the best for you.*

b *The best advice is based on facts.*

d *Advice is someone's opinion.*

f *Advice gives you options.*

2 Once you have decided on an order, check it with another pair. Talk about any differences you have. If you change your mind, change your order.

3 With your partner, write your own definition of what advice is, using ideas from your discussion. Set out your work clearly and neatly as you will return to this definition later in the unit to work on it further.

4 Read your definition out to the rest of the class and listen to other people. Then, if necessary, add more ideas to your own definition.

Purpose and audience

Advice can be given in many different ways depending on the intended purpose and audience. The **purpose** might be to advise someone on how to stop smoking or how to deal with school bullies. The **audience** is the reader or readers for whom the advice is written. This could be adults or children, men or women.

Activity 2

Identify the purpose of the advice and the intended audience in the following texts. Copy the table and fill in the spaces. Think about:
- what the advice is about
- who the advice is being given to
- why the advice is being given.

Text 1

◆ *You can save money and have a lot of fun making bits of fishing gear for yourself.*

Text 2

● The recent ice and snowfalls have made all roads very icy and dangerous. Drivers should not use their cars unless their journey is absolutely necessary.

Text 3

To all Year 6 pupils

WELCOME BACK TO SCHOOL YEAR 6

You are now the oldest pupils in our school and you should act responsibly so that you give a good example to younger ones.

Text 4

Cashmere is a very delicate fabric.
You should remove all jewellery before handling your garment.

Text number	What	Who	Why
1	Make your own fishing gear	Children who like fishing	So they can save money
2			
3			
4			

Investigating informal language

When friends write to each other, they might use the sort of language they use when speaking to each other. This is called **informal language**.

Activity 3

1 Read the two notes on the next page, which have been passed between close friends. Talk about or list examples from the notes, identifying some or all of these features of informal language:

- has a friendly tone
- uses shortened words, for example, *can't, I'll*
- uses short sentences
- uses slang, the vocabulary of everyday speech
- uses nicknames or first names
- uses incomplete sentences.

Note 1

Hiya Beth, do you think I should finish with Mark? Sometimes I want to ... then he looks all helpless and I can't do it!

What are you like?! You know what I think, Shelley. He's a total slob – ditch him!

OK! I'll do it at break.

Way to go!

Note 2

Nick, have you seen how Old Craig keeps picking on me? I'm not the only one messing around but he always goes for me. I hate him! Do you think I should see someone about it?

Yeah, Ben, I know. Loads of us have noticed it. You could try to ignore him but then it might get worse. Perhaps you should say something. Who would listen though?

2 Write a note that might be passed between you and a friend in which your friend asks you for advice about a problem at school. Annotate your note to show how you have used features of informal language. Do you use any other method of communicating with your friends in informal language?

Ways of giving advice

Activity 4

1 In Note 1 the writer gives advice in a direct way, using an imperative (a command): 'Ditch him.' Using imperatives, write two more sentences giving advice to Shelley about her boyfriend. Underline the imperatives.

2 In Note 2 the writer gives advice in a less direct way: 'You could try to ignore him …' adding a warning: '… but then it might get worse.' In this sentence the connective *but* signals a new idea is to follow. Copy and complete the following sentences using the connective *but* to introduce a new idea to the sentence.

a Perhaps you should say something to him *but* …

b You could tell your parents *but* …

3 a Write two different replies to the following note. In one reply give advice directly, using imperatives. In the second reply, give advice indirectly.

HELPPPP! Muppet Man's gonna kill me! I've left my sports kit at home again. Last time he said I'd get detention for a week if it happened again. It's the match tomorrow night as well. I'm dead. What should I do?

b Think about the two different ways of giving advice: directly and indirectly. Is one way more effective than the other? Does it depend on the situation? Give reasons for your answers.

Stages of giving advice

In this section you are going to explore the stages of giving advice.
Read this transcript of a mobile phone conversation between two members of a family.

BEN	Can you hear me? Maybe I should call later when I get off the bus.
MUM	No, it's fine. What's the problem?
BEN	Well, school was a disaster today. I've blown it big time.
MUM	You may be exaggerating things. Nobody from school has phoned, and they generally do.
BEN	I know I shouldn't be so short fused. I mustn't just explode at people, but he made me feel so stupid and useless.
MUM	Listen, OK, shall I pick you up at the stop? We ought to be able to sort this out.

Activity 5

Below are the stages of giving advice. Read them and answer the questions.

Stage 1: Giving reassurance

1 People often want advice when they are upset or worried about something. What do you think Ben is worried about? Give evidence from the conversation above to support your answer.

2 How does Mum reassure Ben and try to make him feel better? Write down two examples from the text and explain why you have chosen them.

Stage 2: Showing you understand the problem

Below is the rest of the conversation, which takes place when Ben gets off the bus.

MUM	Hello dear, how are things now?
BEN	Even worse. Everyone was talking about me on the bus.
MUM	Tell me all about it.
BEN	It started in English when I got some spellings wrong and Lewis laughed at me. Just because he thinks he's a genius, he laughs at everyone else to make them feel stupid. And then in the Science lesson he laughed at me again. So I got out of my seat and threw his book out of the window. And then everyone laughed at me. What am I going to do? I can't go to school tomorrow.
MUM	Well, nobody likes to be laughed at, especially in front of the whole class. You must feel really bad about it all now.

3 Do you think Ben would feel better after this conversation? If so, why?

4 Mum shows she understands Ben's problem by repeating it back to him. Why do you think it is important to show someone you understand their problem before you offer them advice?

Stage 3: Offering advice

5 At this stage, what advice would you give to Ben? Note it down, then read the rest of the conversation.

BEN	I can't go to school tomorrow, I just can't.
MUM	Well, I'm sure it won't be as bad as you think. You could phone Lewis at home or you could talk to him at school tomorrow. If you don't want to speak to him, you could leave a note on his desk. What do you think?
BEN	I'm not sure yet. I'll think about it.

6 What three solutions are offered by Mum? What are the advantages of giving different solutions? Would you choose one of these or something else?

Looking at sentence structure

Two types of sentences are used to offer advice in the conversation above:

- **compound sentences** where two clauses are joined together by a connective such as *or*, *and* and *but*. If the connective were taken away, both clauses would make sense on their own. For example:

  You could phone Lewis at home tonight.   You could talk to him at school tomorrow.

  You could phone Lewis at home tonight **OR** talk to him at school tomorrow.

  When giving advice, using a compound sentence is a good way of offering choices.

- **complex sentences** which have a main clause and a subordinate clause. The main clause makes sense on its own, but the subordinate clause needs to be part of a longer sentence to make complete sense. For example:

  subordinate clause   main clause
  If you don't want to speak to him, you could leave a note on his desk.

  By starting a sentence with *if* you can point out what might happen, but still let the other person make up their own mind. This is a useful technique for giving advice.

Activity 6

1 To practise using compound sentences write a piece of advice for a friend with each of these problems.

- I've left my homework at home again. What should I do?
- I've taken a CD from my brother's room and now I've lost it. Should I tell him?

Remember to offer alternative pieces of advice using the connectives *and/or/but*.

2 Practise using *if* in complex sentences by copying and completing these sentences.

  a *If* you do this straightaway, _____ .

  b *If* you tackle the problem by speaking to her face to face, _____ .

  c *If* you stay behind after school, _____ .

Sharpen spelling

Double letters

To remember when to use a double or single letter in the middle of a word, there are two helpful techniques.

Visualise the word

- Write down the word several times.
- Close your eyes and visualise the word.
- Write it down again.

Try this with 'embarrass' and 'committee'.

Syllabification

- Break the tricky word into syllables (units of sound).
- Say each syllable out loud, for example: 'exaggerating' = ex + agg + er + at + ing.
- Say the word aloud several times.
- Try writing down the whole word.

Try this with 'dissolve' and 'accommodation'.

Offering your own advice

You are going to use what you have learnt so far in this unit to improvise (make up) a conversation with a partner. Your improvisation will be based on a parent offering a child some advice.

Activity 7

1 Make some notes to help you plan your conversation before you begin. Do **not** write out the conversation in full. The idea of an improvisation is that you respond naturally to what your partner says.

2 Follow these stages in your improvised conversation:

- explain feelings
- offer reassurance
- explain the problem in detail
- try to include one piece of advice that begins with the phrase *If you …*

Child
Explain your feelings

Parent
Offer reassurance

Child
Explain the problem in detail

Parent
Offer more than one piece of advice.
Use the phrases: *You could …* and *If you …*

Feedback

When you have practised your improvisation, perform it for another pair of students. Ask them to put a tick every time they hear you include one of the points on the bullet point list above. How many ticks did you score? The maximum you can score is four. When you have your score, think about whether you could have tackled anything better. Talk with your partner about improvements you could make.

 Progress check

Look back at the learning you have done so far in this unit. You have:
- discussed the meaning of advice
- searched a text for examples of informal language
- thought about the stages of giving advice
- examined the use of compound and complex sentences in advice
- improvised a conversation giving advice.

1 Write down the two things you have done best and draw a star by them.

2 Write two things down you need to learn more about and draw an arrow beside them. Write a sentence explaining why you feel unsure about them.

Formal advice

Teachers will often give students advice informally, perhaps at the end of a lesson or in form time. At other times, in Assembly for example, the advice is given in a more formal way.

 Activity 8
Read the Assembly speech on the next page given by a Year Head. The notes show you how the talk has been organised.

> Year Seven, it has only been a short time since the beginning of term and you've had many new things to come to terms with. It can be quite a frightening experience at first, but by now you should all know that secondary schools are busy, complicated places.

Speaker tells students he understands how they feel.

> Nobody could possibly keep in their heads all the things that need to be done. You need to remember your timetable, your homework, your teachers' names, as well as find your way around. This is why we supply you all with a planner at the start of each year.

Speaker shows he understands the problem by focusing on the difficulties they have.

> Every student ought to learn how to organise their time efficiently. Planning for the week ahead should be part of everyone's weekend agenda.

Speaker gives a particular piece of advice.

> A lazy approach to personal organisation will not be tolerated at this school. We all need to achieve. Therefore, we must all organise our time effectively.

Speaker reinforces the advice.

Using a formal tone

The tone of a piece of writing can change according to the **audience** (the reader or listener). It can also change according to the **purpose** (the reason for writing). The Assembly speech uses a formal tone. The main features of formal language are:

- it uses standard English, not slang
- it uses vocabulary not always used in everyday speech, for example, 'tolerated'.

Activity 9

1 Explain why formal language is used in this talk. Think about:
- the audience (the people who are listening to the message)
- the purpose (the reason why the message is being delivered).

2 The tone of this advice is more formal than other advice covered in this unit. It does not sound like the language used in everyday speech. Rewrite the last paragraph of the Assembly speech in informal language.

Using pronouns

You are going to look closely at the pronouns *you* and *we* used in the Assembly speech (page 115).

A pronoun is a word that stands in for the name of a person or object. For example, you could say 'John kicked the ball' or 'he kicked the ball'. Here the pronoun is *he*.

Activity 10

1 To help you understand when and why certain pronouns are used:
- count and record how many times *you* and *we* are used
- identify who the speaker is referring to when he says *you all*
- identify who the speaker is referring to when he says *we*
- think about what the speaker hopes to achieve by saying 'We must all plan our time carefully'.

2 Do you think the use of the pronoun *we* is successful in the Assembly speech? Give reasons for your answer.

Writing your own advice

You are going to write your own advice for Year 7 students.

Activity 11

1 Choose a topic you know they might need advice about, for example: homework, being on time for lessons, finding their way around school.

2 Aim to write four short paragraphs. Follow this outline:

Paragraph 1: Show students that you understand their experience.
Paragraph 2: Give the students your first piece of advice.
Paragraph 3: Give the students your second piece of advice.
Paragraph 4: Summarise your advice.

3 To make sure your writing is successful remember to:
- use a formal tone so that you sound like a teacher
- use standard English, not slang
- address your audience using the pronoun *you*
- use the pronoun *we* in your summary so that the students feel they are all trying to achieve the same thing.

Feedback

1 Read your finished text aloud to another student. If they think you sound like a head teacher or a head of year, then you have done a good job!

2 Ask a partner to give you feedback on your talk using these success criteria.
   a Was the talk well organised? Did it follow the outline above?
   b Were the pronouns *you* and *we* used to address students?
   c Was the vocabulary formal enough?

3 Ask your partner to choose one area where your work could be improved.
   Here are some examples of comments you might want to make when giving feedback to another student.
   • That was really good. You sound just like my head of year!
   • I think you need to add some more formal vocabulary such as 'disappointing' or 'expectations'.
   • Your sentences need to be longer. This sounds a bit like a chat between friends.

Using modal verbs

When you write advice you often use modal verbs. These are verbs that stand alongside a main verb. They are used when you want to suggest that something could possibly happen, which is why they are useful when giving advice.
The modal verbs are: *would, should, might, may, must, ought to, can, could, will.*

Activity 12

1 Look at these examples. For each sentence identify the modal verb and explain the effect on the person receiving the advice.
   • You must do your homework straightaway.
   • You could do your homework now.

2 a Which modal verbs do you think would be most useful when giving advice? Why?
   b Which ones would you avoid when giving advice because they sound too bossy? Why?

3 Copy this text. It is the first paragraph of an advice leaflet for Year 7 students on bullying. Fill in each gap with a suitable modal verb.

Sometimes students worry when they come to a new school because they think they _____ get bullied. If you have any worries about bullying there are several things you _____ do. First, you _____ tell a teacher or an older student. What is certain is that you _____ not suffer in silence.

4 Compare your text with another student's and explain your choices.

5 You are going to continue the text for two or three more paragraphs, giving specific advice to students who may be bullied in school.

a First work with a partner to make a list of advice you could include, for example, walk home with a friend, how to stand up to bullies.

b Then write your advice. Remember to:
- use formal language
- reassure students that someone will help them
- show understanding of the problem
- use a range of pronouns
- offer suggestions to help them cope with bullying
- use modal verbs.

Feedback

1 Check a partner's first draft. Make sure your partner has:
a reassured the readers that someone will help
b shown understanding of the problem
c included a range of suggestions
d used modal verbs and pronouns appropriately.

Write the correct letter in the margin of your partner's work to show where they have included the features on the checklist. Show your partner where they could make improvements.

2 Mark on your draft the places where you need to make improvements before you make changes. Then write your final draft.

Progress check

1 Remind yourself of the work you have done so far in this unit on giving advice. Write one sentence about each of these items:
   a the type of language you can use (formal or informal)
   b when to use it
   c the correct tone to adopt to make sure your readers or listeners take your advice
   d how to begin and end advice
   e the types of sentences and modal verbs you could use.

2 Add any of your own ideas about giving advice. If you are not sure about any of the points on the list above, ask a partner to help you out.

3 Now write a short paragraph with the title: 'How to make your advice count'. Your audience is teachers. You should tell them what you think they need to know when giving advice to their students.

Professional advice on websites

So far you have looked at advice from people you know and who give you advice face to face. Professional providers of advice, unlike friends, families and schools, rarely get to see their audience face to face as they usually write in newspapers, magazines and on the Internet. Their approach has to be direct and personal, but it also has to appeal to large numbers of people.

Activity 13
1 a Copy the statements below about getting advice from a website.
  b Write 'agree' or 'disagree' next to each one.
  c Add some more statements of your own about the advantages and disadvantages of getting advice from a website.

> Websites don't work because you need to speak to someone face to face.

> You don't know the person giving the advice, so you can't trust them.

> Websites might not be reliable.

> Websites are confidential. No one knows if you are using one for advice.

> Websites contain the most up-to-date information.

> Website advice can be presented in an interesting way with links for readers to follow.

2 Decide whether each statement is an advantage or a disadvantage of using a website for professional advice. Sort the statements using a table like the one below and give reasons for your choice. Some statements might fall into both columns, for different reasons.

Using websites for advice	
Advantages	**Disadvantages**

Highlight thinking

Taking a balanced view
When considering advantages and disadvantages, it is useful to:
- keep an open mind
- think from different points of view
- list advantages and disadvantages
- notice areas that don't fall neatly into one or the other – these are often the most 'interesting' ones to explore further.
- balance the pros and cons when coming to a conclusion.

How websites attract attention

To be successful professional advisers need first to attract and then hold the attention of their readers. Above all, this kind of advice needs to know its audience. It needs to:
- focus on the right kind of topics
- provide just the right level of advice for its readers
- use the right sort of language to appeal to readers.

Activity 14
Look at the webpage from the ChildLine website on the opposite page and answer the questions around it. How does the page:
- a attract and appeal to readers
- b adopt the right tone
- c include suitable topics for its audience?

Evaluating the website
An evaluation is an explanation of what works well and what doesn't. When you write an evaluation you should point out the good and bad points of something and decide how effective it is. You should take into account audience and purpose.

1 Why is the telephone placed at the top of the page?

2 What words are used to reassure young people? Why is this sentence in bold type?

3 Why have cartoon characters been used?

4 What information in this box would encourage children to use the website?

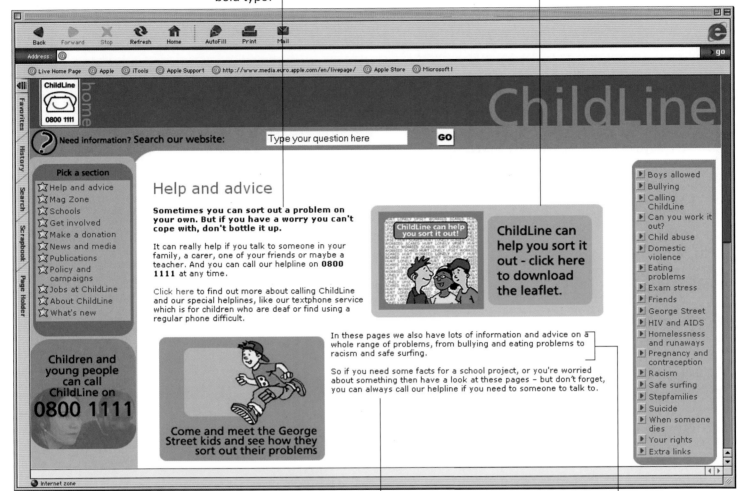

5 What colours have been used? What effect does this have?

6 What tone is adopted here? Is it formal or informal? Why do you think this tone has been used?

7 Do you think these are suitable topics for a young person's problem page?

Activity 15

1 Produce a short evaluation of the ChildLine website. Write six to eight lines and include answers to the following questions. You could discuss your ideas with a partner before you begin writing.

   a How do the design and layout of the website attract readers? (Refer to the use of colour, pictures and the way the ideas are arranged.)

   b How does the tone of the language suggest that readers will get suitable advice from this website? For example, does it sound helpful and friendly? (Give specific examples from the text.)

   c Would this webpage encourage readers to explore the site further? (Give reasons and examples to support your answer.)

2 When you have finished, show your work to another student and compare your ideas. Is there anything else you can add to your work?

Feedback

1 Read through your evaluation of the website. Decide which of the following statements best matches your ability to do this task.
   - I wasn't sure at all about how to write the evaluation. (red)
   - There were one or two places where I was unsure. (amber)
   - I had no problems with the evaluation. I knew exactly what to do. (green)

2 If you gave yourself a red or amber light you need to do these things.
   a Write down the specific areas where you had difficulty, for example, 'I didn't know how to answer the last question on the list' or 'I wasn't sure how to comment on the way the ideas were arranged'.
   b Ask a student who had a green light to show you how they tackled these points.
   c Ask your teacher to give you a support sheet to help you improve your paragraph.

Responding to an advice column

On the opposite page are some extracts from ChildLine's Agony Uncle in which he provides professional advice to some boys who have written to him.

Activity 16

1 With a partner, skim read these three pieces of professional advice. By skim reading, you are aiming to get a quick overview of the texts. Now answer the questions below. Remember, when you are asked to explain your answers, you should:
   - give reasons to support your opinions
   - refer to examples from the text
   - speak clearly and confidently.

   a This advice page is aimed at boys. Do you think these questions would appeal to both boys and girls? Give reasons for your answer.
   b Advice websites have to interest their readers as well as helping them. Which piece of advice do you find the most interesting? Explain why.
   c Which piece of advice do you think was the most useful and which was the least useful? Give reasons for your answers.
   d Do you think the advice given on this website is reliable? Why or why not?

Address: @

Live Home Page | Apple | iTools | Apple Support | http://www.media.euro.apple.com/en/livepage/ | Apple Store | Microsoft MacTopia | MSN | Office for Macintosh | Internet Explorer

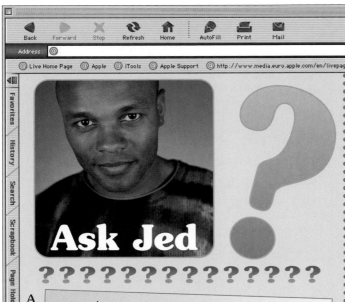

Ask Jed

? ? ? ? ? ? ? ? ? ? ? ? ?

A

I got into a fight recently when an older boy started saying bad stuff about me. The school says fighting is wrong but my dad says I have to stick up for myself. I'm confused – aren't boys meant to be tough?

Boys can be tough in lots of ways. Fighting is not the answer to your problems as it will only get you into trouble and won't solve anything. You can stand your ground by telling this older boy that what he's saying is wrong and that you aren't scared of him. If you think he may try to attack you try making sure you are always in a group of friends and make sure a teacher knows that there is a problem.

? ? ? ? ? ? ? ? ? ? ? ? ?

B

Why do girls get away with laughing at boys at school – but if I say something about girls I get into trouble for being sexist? Boys just seem to get put down all the time – like in TV ads – that can't be right can it?

OK. Just so you know – there's a lot of history behind this one that's far too complicated to go into now. Maybe you could get a debate going about this issue in pastoral care or through the school council. That said, the bottom line is that no one should have to put up with verbal abuse however trivial it may seem. Remember, if anyone, girl or boy, is saying stuff that is upsetting to someone else then that's bullying – and your school has a responsibility to take it seriously and not let them get away with it.

? ? ? ? ? ? ? ? ? ? ? ?

C

Sometimes I feel like talking to my mates about my troubles at home – but I know they'll laugh. Do you reckon they worry about stuff as well?

You won't be the only one with problems – but sometimes even good mates can find it hard to talk about really personal stuff. Maybe there's someone in your group of mates who you can trust not to go blabbing to the others? Even then it depends how serious the problem is. Arguing about schoolwork is annoying but something most people can relate to. On the other hand talking about the fact that, for example, your dad gets drunk and hits your brother is way more serious and you may want to consider talking to a trusted adult or an organisation who can offer professional advice and support – like ChildLine.

Internet zone

2 Work in small groups to discuss your ideas about the questions above.

3 Work with a partner and explain your answers. When you do this, make sure you have an example from the text to support your point of view. To find the examples, you will have to read the texts again closely.

Language in advice texts

You are going to look at the way in which language is used in advice texts. The writer of Extracts A–C has matched the language of his text to the needs of his audience (young people). He has used a friendly tone by using informal language. He writes as if he is speaking directly to his audience.

Activity 17

1 a Copy and complete the table below to work out:

- where the writer uses informal language
- the effect it has on the reader.

b Give one example of your own from each extract. An example is given to help you get started.

Extract	Example of informal language	Effect on the reader
Extract A	You can stand your own ground	Will give the reader confidence
Extract B		
Extract C		

Sharpen spelling

Adding -ing

When you add the suffix -ing to a word you usually add it directly to the base word, for example: look ⟶ look*ing*

If there is one short vowel between two consonants, you double the consonant before you add -ing, for example:

skip ⟶ skipp*ing*

If the base word ends in a single e, drop the -e before adding -ing, for example:

hate ⟶ hat*ing*

1 Read through Extracts A to C again noting all the words that end in -ing.

2 Copy and complete this table to show how the words add the suffix -ing.

Words that do not change the spelling of the base word before adding -ing	Words that double the consonant before adding -ing	Words that drop the -e before adding -ing

Sharpen punctuation

Dashes

1 Look again at the requests for advice on page 123. A dash is used once in Extract A. Try to work out why a dash has been used here. It may help you to read the letter aloud to find the answer.

2 Now look at this example from Extract B.

Boys just seem to get put down all the time – like in TV ads – that can't be right can it?

Work out the reason for the two dashes here.

3 The reply in Extract C ends with a phrase introduced by a dash – like ChildLine. What is the reason for this dash?

Writing your own advice texts for a website

You are going to write some advice of your own.

Activity 18

1 Begin by writing a request for advice. Choose one of the problems from the bubbles below or think of your own.

Remember, when you are writing your own advice text:
- keep your request for help short – not more than three or four lines
- begin by explaining the problem (make sure it's true to life)
- make your final sentence a request for help
- use informal language and aim to sound as if you are speaking to someone face to face
- use at least one dash to show a pause or that something extra has been added to the sentence.

2 When you have finished, check your work. Make sure you have followed the checklist above about writing advice texts.

3 Exchange your work with a partner and write a reply to your partner's request for advice.

When you are writing your reply remember to:
- begin by reassuring your reader
- show you understand their problem
- remember to offer more than one piece of advice so the reader can make a choice
- use informal language, as if you are talking to your reader
- include modal verbs such as could, can, might, may.

Feedback

1 When you read your partner's reply to your request for advice, decide how helpful it is by asking yourself the following questions.
   a Is the tone informal?
   b Does the reply offer reassurance first?
   c Is the advice sensible and realistic?
   d Do they use modal verbs to offer advice?

2 Now look back at the two pieces of writing you have done – your own request for advice and the reply to your partner's request for advice. Identify two ways in which you could improve your pieces of writing. Use the checklists on page 125 to help you.

Influencing readers

When you advise someone, you offer them choices. Your aim is to help them. Sometimes writers try to help readers in a more direct way by persuading them. You are going to look at a text that aims to persuade readers to think carefully about smoking and its effects.

 Activity 19

1 Before you explore the text on smoking, think about:
   a why people smoke
   b how smoking affects other people and their environment.

   Working with a partner, copy and complete this spidergram with your ideas.

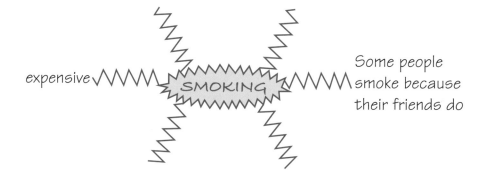

2 Read the text on the next page. It is from a magazine article persuading readers to join its anti-smoking campaign. As you read, answer the questions so that you can begin to understand some of the methods the writer uses to persuade readers.

SMOKING SUCKS!

Cool as your pa's pants!

If we told you there was a wicked new craze that would take up all of your pocket money, make you smell bad AND make you ill, you'd NEVER agree it was cool. So why would you wanna puff?

Here's the deal ...

Over 120,000 people died in the UK last year cos of cigarettes. Surveys show that 1 in 20 of 13-year-olds smoke at least one a week. That's why we've started on our anti-smoking campaign. And we want you to join in. Still not convinced? Then read on ...

How does the tone becomes more serious here?

Strong positive language.

Explain how facts and figures are used to persuade readers.

> Killing yourself to look cool is sooo not smart. So use your brain and join the Mizz anti-smoking campaign ...

What language does the writer use to target the reader? How is it effective?

It's unfair

If you sat in a restaurant with a smoker, you'd inhale so much of their smoke, it'd be like you'd puffed TWO cigarettes yourself. How horrible is that? Smoking in public places is still legal in the UK. Though lots of anti-smoking groups are campaigning to stop it. So tell your puffing parents they're harming you AND themselves. And tell 'em off if they light up near you.

It's addictive

It's so easy to get hooked on smoking. Some experts even think that nicotine, the chemical you get in cigarettes, is even more addictive than dangerous drugs than cocaine. If you smoke, then give up, it takes 15 YEARS for your body to repair itself back to the state of someone who's never smoked.

It's illegal

If you're under 16 and were sold fags in a shop, then the shopkeeper would be breaking the law. The Children and Young Persons Act of 1933 (yup, it's that ancient!) makes it a criminal offence to sell ciggies to anyone under the age of 16. Which means a shopkeeper could be fined up to £2,500 if they're caught selling a packet to you.

Smoking myths

How do the answers to the comments persuade readers not to smoke?

'SMOKING'S NOT THAT EXPENSIVE'
Yes it is! If you smoked one fag a day for five years, it'd cost you a whopping £400.

'I ONLY SMOKE OCCASIONALLY SO IT'S NOT DANGEROUS'
Listen up. If you start smoking, each fag can take up to FIVE MINUTES off your life. A pack of 20 = two episodes of *Hollyoaks*. How not worth it is that?

How does the use of humour engage readers?

'SMOKING CHILLS YOU OUT.'
Uh-huh! The nicotine you get in fags actually makes your heartbeat race. And that's not relaxing is it?

'LIGHT FAGS ARE HEALTHIER THAN NORMAL ONES'
Low-tar cigarettes are just as bad as the regular ones. Because smokers inhale them more deeply, they get just as many bad chemicals as with harsher fags.

Presentation of persuasive texts

The article on smoking has been designed for an audience of young people with the purpose of influencing and persuading them. To attract the attention of their readers, the writers make the text look interesting and easy to read. They have done this by:

- using background colour
- organising the page layout so that the information is split up.

Activity 20

1 Look at the article again to work out how the writers have attracted your attention. Now look at the table below and match the background colour and shapes on the left with the part of the text where they are used.

Sharpen spelling

Prefixes

Find the word *illegal* in the text. It is made up of the prefix *il-* and the word *legal*.

A prefix is a group of letters that is added to the front of the base word to change its meaning. Putting the prefix *il-* in front of a word gives the word an opposite meaning. That means *legal* (lawful) becomes *illegal* (unlawful) when *il-* is put in front of it.

If the last letter of the prefix is the same as the first letter of the base word, you just double up the letter, as in *illegal*.

Three more prefixes that give a word an opposite meaning are: *un- dis- mis-*

Write down five examples for each prefix. Use a dictionary to help you if you wish.

blue background	presents facts about smoking
white background/box	presents readers' own words
purple background	introduces topic of smoking
circle with black background	introduces campaign
circle with red background	corrects wrong ideas about smoking

2 Now answer these questions.
  a How have the writers divided up the information on the page into small sections?
  b Why do you think they have done this? (Think about the amount of information they are trying to get across to their readers.)
  c What other ways can you spot in which the writers have tried to make the page look interesting to attract the attention of their readers?
  d In your opinion, have the writers been successful in attracting your attention and interest? Give reasons for your answer.

Fact and opinion

To influence the way readers think, writers use a combination of facts and opinion. **Facts** are statements that are true. They can help to persuade readers because they provide evidence and information. These statements are facts.

- There are 30 chairs in this classroom. (This could be proved by counting the chairs.)
- In a recent survey, 58 per cent of Year 7 students said they get too much homework. (This could be proved by checking the survey.)

Opinions relate to what somebody believes or thinks. They express a point of view. These statements are opinions.

- My classroom needs better furniture. (This is someone's point of view.)
- I hate doing homework. (This is what someone thinks.)

The article on smoking uses both facts and opinions.

 **Activity 21**

1 a Look closely at 'Smoking myths' in the article on page 127.
The statements in the black circles are opinions. They are based on what some people believe about smoking and are not necessarily true. The replies are facts because they are based on scientific research and can be proved to be true.

- 'SMOKING'S NOT THAT EXPENSIVE'
- 'I ONLY SMOKE OCCASIONALLY SO IT'S NOT DANGEROUS'
- 'SMOKING CHILLS YOU OUT.'
- 'LIGHT FAGS ARE HEALTHIER THAN NORMAL ONES'

b Look closely at the statements from the article. Copy them out and decide whether they are facts or opinions. Write F or O next to each statement.

- Smoking sucks!
- Smoking in public places is still legal in the UK.
- Killing yourself to look cool is sooo not smart.

2 Work with a partner to find two more facts and two more opinions in the article.

3 Write one sentence in which you express your own opinion of smoking.

SMOKING SUCKS!

Using language to get attention

The writer has used a range of language and punctuation techniques to attract the reader's attention.

Activity 22

1 Copy and complete the table below with examples from the text. Use the list on the right to refresh your memory about the techniques.

- **Alliteration:** words beginning with the same sound.
- **Repetition:** words or phrases used more than once, usually placed close together.
- **Pun:** where writers play with words that have more than one meaning.
- **Simile:** a comparison, usually using the words *as* or *like*.

Technique	Example	Effect on the reader
Alliteration	Smoking sucks	Helps reader to remember key message
Repetition		
Simile		
Pun		
Exclamation mark		
Question mark		

2 Write your own statements about smoking using the techniques above.

Exploring informal language

Magazines are read by large numbers of young people. One reason for their popularity is that they use the kind of informal language that young people use every day. Magazine writers want readers to feel that reading a magazine is like having a chat with a friend.

Activity 23

1 Look closely at this extract from the article on smoking (page 127) where informal language is used.

> **Smoking sucks!**
> Cool as your pa's pants!
> If we told you there was a wicked new craze that would take up all of your pocket money, make you smell bad AND make you ill, you'd NEVER agree it was cool. So why would you wanna puff?

Rewrite this text in formal language, as if you were writing for an adult audience. Remember that not all adults would understand the language used in the magazine, so you will have to think of alternatives, for example, 'smoking is not a good thing' (smoking sucks).

2 a 'Smoking sucks!' is a persuasion text. Persuasion texts:

- are written in the present tense
- use facts and opinions to convince readers
- use strong, positive language
- are able to make readers feel everyone does this or agrees with this
- use techniques such as alliteration to make ideas memorable
- are humorous in places to get readers on their side.

With a partner, look back at the text on page 127 to check where these features are used.

Writing your own persuasion text

Activity 24

You are going to design and write a page for an anti-litter campaign called 'Stop now!' Your audience is young people aged between eleven and fifteen. Your purpose is to draw attention to the problem of litter in schools and to make people think before they drop litter. You should draw attention to the effect of litter on the school environment.

Step 1

Study this fact file.

WASTE FACTS

- In an average secondary school one ton of rubbish is collected every month.

- There are £30 million worth of aluminium drinks cans in the UK waiting to be collected, cashed in and recycled.

- Each person in the UK throws away seven times their body weight in rubbish every year.

- Every year in the UK the rat population increases (because rats feed on rubbish).

- Urban foxes consuming rubbish have been found on school premises.

Step 2

Decide which information you will use in your writing and the order in which you will use it. Are there any other details you could include?

Step 3

Plan how you will set the information out on the page and what background colours you will use. Do not do any detailed colouring at this stage.

Step 4

Decide how you will make the information stand out. For example, will you place some information in boxes or use underlining?

Step 5

Use your knowledge of the features of writing to persuade to plan your first draft. Remember your audience is young people so you should use an informal tone and the vocabulary young people use.

Step 6

When you have finished your first draft, highlight and name all the features of writing to persuade you have used.

Step 7

Show your draft to a partner and ask them to help you to add more of these features, if necessary. Ask your partner to check your language, would your text appeal to young people?

Step 8

When you have made changes to your first draft, write your final copy. Colour should be added at this stage as well as presentational techniques such as highlighting, underlining and placing information in boxes.

✓ Progress check

Now you have completed your persuasion text, assess your progress by copying the chart below and colouring in the sections. Use this colour coding:

Red = I struggled with this. I would like some more help to improve.

Amber = There are still some things I am not quite sure about.

Green = I am very confident about this task.

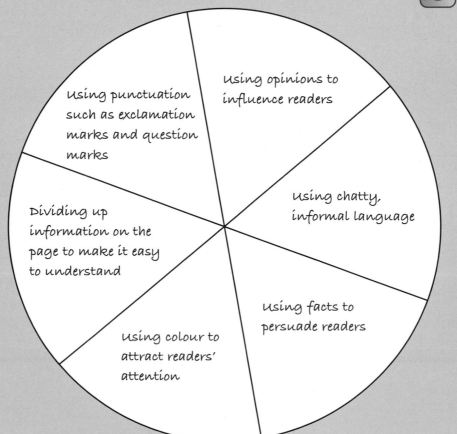

⬭ Assessment task

Look at the following webpages from Battersea Dogs' Home. You will make your own notes before writing an evaluation of the website. You need to show you can:

- identify the purpose and the audience
- identify the presentational features and explain their effects
- identify how language is used to influence the reader
- evaluate the text.

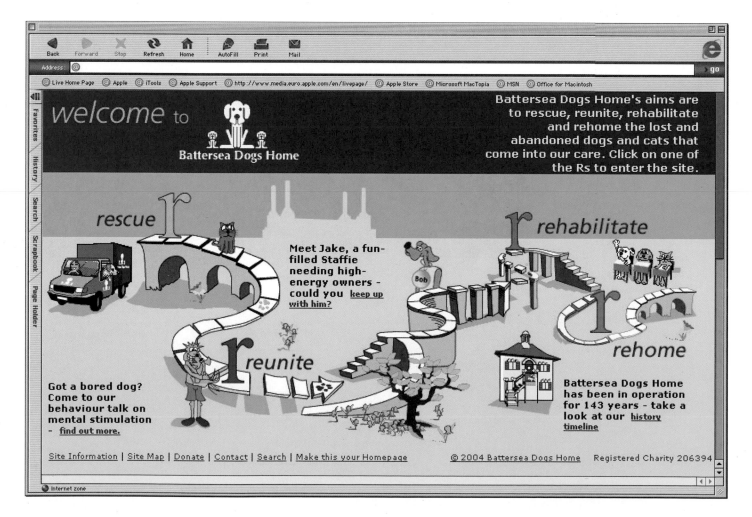

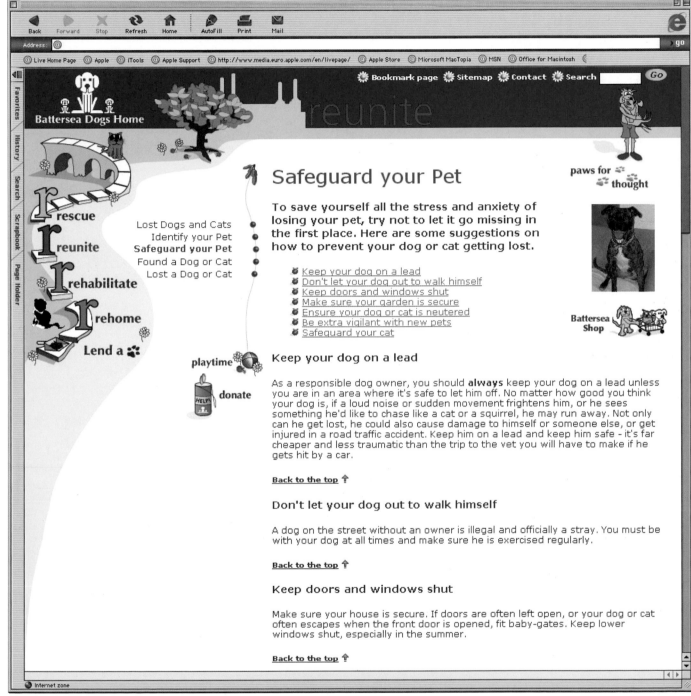

Study the web pages again carefully and make notes under each of these headings. Remember when you make notes you should write very briefly; you do **not** need to write in full sentences. You can use bullet points to help you separate items in a list.

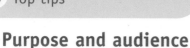

Purpose and audience

- Look closely at the webpages and make a list of reasons why the website has been produced.
- Think about the intended audience for this website. Who would be interested in reading about the dogs' home?

Presentational features

- How have the designers used colour to attract their audience?
- How have the designers used pictures? Think about the cartoon pictures as well as the photograph. What effect would each of these have on readers?
- How have the designers made sure that readers will want to continue reading their website?
- How have they used the words *rescue, reunite, rehabilitate, rehome*?

Use of language

- Does the website use formal or informal language?
- The website uses the pronoun *you* quite often. Explain the effect this would have on readers.
- Find examples of imperatives and explain why the designers have used them on the second page.
- Find examples of modal verbs and explain the effect on readers when these verbs are used.

Evaluation

Now you are ready to put your notes together to write your evaluation. Look back to page 121 to remind yourself of how to approach this. Re-read the evaluation you wrote on the ChildLine website. Remember an evaluation is an explanation of what works well and what doesn't. Point out the good and bad points of the Battersea Dogs' Home website and say whether you think it is effective. Explain your reasons.

You should write about:

- intended purpose and audience
- how the design/layout would/would not attract readers
- how language is used to keep readers reading
- how the home page encourages readers to explore further.

Write your first draft using the notes you made. When you have finished read your work and use the headings above to make sure you have included everything. Make any changes you think are necessary before you write the final draft.

6 Fantastic fiction

The bigger picture

In this unit you will explore how a writer uses language and narrative techniques to involve and entertain a reader in a longer text.

The unit is based around the award-winning novel *Artemis Fowl* by Irish writer, Eoin Colfer. The book has been described as *'Fantastic stuff from beginning to end ... a rip-roaring, 21st-century romp of the highest order ... what we have here is well written, sophisticated, rough 'n' tumble storytelling with enough high-octane attitude to make it a seriously cool read...'*

At the end of the unit you will respond to a text by commenting on the writer's use of language, then produce a short piece of your own writing that uses some of these techniques.

WHAT? You will:
- explore how a writer creates and develops character and setting
- investigate a range of techniques used by a writer to grip the reader
- identify and comment on a writer's ideas

HOW? by:
- using a range of reading techniques
- analysing a writer's use of language
- experimenting with writing techniques

WHY? because:
- reading is a rewarding experience
- investigation through reading helps you with your own writing
- reading closely makes you think more deeply and helps you to develop your personal response

Understanding genre

There are many different types of story. Each type is a genre. We generally recognise different story genres by clues the writer gives us in:

- what the story is about
- the way it is written.

Activity 1

1 Draw a spidergram naming as many different types of story as you can.

2 List some features of the fairy tale genre. Think about:

- how fairy tales start and end
- the types of characters in fairy tales
- animals in fairy tales
- what happens to the 'baddie'.

3 Here are seven extracts from *Artemis Fowl* (1–7). With a partner, match them to the texts from other well-known books and films (a–g). Name the genres of each match. You could write your answers in a table like this:

Extract	Text	Genre
1	f	Detective

1

'But, sir, I am the waiter.'

Artemis tapped the table for attention.

'You are wearing handmade loafers, a silk shirt and three gold signet rings. Your English has a tinge of Oxford about it and your nails have the soft sheen of
5 the recently manicured. You are not a waiter. You are our contact, Nguyen Xuan, and you have adopted this pathetic disguise to discreetly check for weaponry.'

Nguyen's shoulders sagged. 'It is true. Amazing.'

2

'What's that?'

'It's a finger. What does it look like?'

'A finger,' admitted Root.

'Yes, but not any ordinary finger.' He
5 glanced around to make sure that no one
else was watching. 'The tip contains a
pressurised dart. One shot only. You tap
the knuckle with your thumb and someone
goes sleepy-bye.'

3

Dwarfs did not like fire. They didn't even
like thinking about flames. Unlike the rest
of the fairy races, dwarfs had no desire to
live above ground.

4

Holly drew her weapon and flicked it up to
the second setting. She couldn't kill the
troll under any circumstances. Not to save
humans. But she could certainly put him
5 out until Retrieval arrived.

Aiming for the weak point at the base of
the skull, she let the troll have a long burst
of the concentrated ion ray.

5

The troll was directly below her, pounding
against the town's outer wall, which was
coming away in chunks beneath his
powerful fingers.

6

The pod's clamp tilted, rolling Holly into the
abyss. Her stomach tightened as G-force
took hold, dragging her to the centre of the
earth. The seismology section had a million
5 probes down here, with a 99.8 success
rate at predicting the magma flares.

7

Finally the coast loomed ahead of her. The
old country, Éiriú, the land where time
began. The most magical place on the
planet. It was here, 10,000 years ago, that
5 the ancient fairy race, the Dé Danann, had
battled against the demon Formorians,
carving the famous Giant's Causeway with
the strength of their magical blasts. It was
here that the Lia Fáil stood, the rock at the
10 centre of the universe, where the fairy kings
and later the human Ard Rí were crowned.

a

b

c

Q: Now this one I'm particularly keen about. You see the gear lever here? Now, if you take the top off, you will find a little red button. Whatever you do, don't touch it.

Bond: Yeah, why not?

Q: Because you'll release this section of the roof, and engage and then fire the passenger ejector seat.
Whish!

d

I am afraid I cannot convey the peculiar sensations of time travelling. They are excessively unpleasant. There is a feeling exactly like that on has upon a switchback – of a helpless headlong motion! I felt the same horrible anticipation, too, of an imminent smash. As I put on pace, night followed day like the flapping of a black wing.

e

Yet it is clear that Hobbits had, in fact, lived quietly in Middle-earth for many long years before other folk became even aware of them. And the world being after all full of strange creatures beyond count, these little people seemed of very little importance.

f

'I perceive also that whoever addressed the envelope had to go and inquire as to the address.'

'How can you tell that?'

'The name, you see, is in perfectly black ink, which has dried itself. The rest is of the greyish colour which shows that blotting-paper has been used. If it had been written straight off, and then blotted, none would be of a deep black shade. This man has written the name, and there has been a pause before he wrote the address, which can only mean that he was not familiar with it.'

g

Artemis Fowl is a book that draws on a range of genres. Look back over the extracts on pages 138–40. Talk about what kind of book you think this is going to be. Here are some words and phrases that might help your discussions.

mysterious   filled with adventure   make believe

exciting   lots of baddies   *Full of Fantasy*   **funny**

Feedback

Check you have understood the work on genre by quickly writing the answers to these questions.

1 What is meant by the term 'genre'?

2 Name five genres of story.

3 Identify at least three features of one genre you named.

If you cannot answer all three questions, look back over pages 138–40.

Exploring openings

The opening of a book often give clues about the kind of genre it is, and the kinds of worlds and characters the reader might meet. *Artemis Fowl* opens with a prologue.

Openings

Read the prologue to *Artemis Fowl* closely and complete Activity 2.

Prologue

How does one describe Artemis Fowl? Various psychiatrists have tried and failed. The main problem is Artemis's own intelligence. He bamboozles every test thrown at him. He has puzzled the greatest medical minds and sent many of them gibbering to their own hospitals.

5   There is no doubt that Artemis is a child prodigy. But why does someone of such brilliance dedicate himself to criminal activities? This is a question that can be answered by only one person. And he delights in not talking.

Perhaps the best way to create an accurate picture of Artemis is to tell the by now famous account of his first villainous venture. I have put together this
10 report from first-hand interviews with the victims, and as the tale unfolds you will realise that this was not easy.

The story began several years ago at the dawn of the twenty-first century. Artemis Fowl had devised a plan to restore his family's fortune. A plan that could topple civilisations and plunge the planet into a cross-species war.

15   He was twelve years old at the time …

Activity 2

1 Below are some statements about the viewpoint the writer takes in the prologue. Do you agree or disagree with these statements? For each one, give your reason(s).

  a He writes as though he knows Artemis.

  b He writes as though he's a medical expert.

  c He writes as though it's a true story.

  d He writes as though it's a fairy story.

  e He writes as though it happened a long time ago.

  f He writes as though he's in the story.

2 The prologue gives us clues about Artemis and what will happen in the story. Copy and complete this table to help you predict what kinds of things will happen. Add clues to the first column and say what the clues suggest in the second column.

Sharpen spelling

Words that end in -logue

1 Look up these words in a dictionary. Make a note of:

  a their meaning

  b the origin of each word.

    catalogue   dialogue

    epilogue   monologue

2 Which letters in the ending of each word are not pronounced?

3 Use what you have discovered about the words above to guess what the word 'prologue' means. Then check your guess in your dictionary.

Clues	What the clues suggest
He has puzzled the greatest medical minds.	That he is very clever and maybe that he has been captured and investigated.
But why does someone of such brilliance dedicate himself to criminal activities?	

3 On page 141 you talked about what kind of book you thought *Artemis Fowl* would be. Using those ideas and what you have discovered from the prologue, write a paragraph to explain:

  a what you think the book will be about   b why you think this.

Setting the scene

In the first chapter of a book, a writer uses different techniques to set the scene for what's to follow. You are going to explore how a writer's use of similes, verbs, adverbs and adjectives help to set the scene.

Use of language to set a scene

In Chapter 1 of *Artemis Fowl*, the world of fairies and the world of man meet.

You are going to explore different techniques a writer uses to present the next scene and the most unusual character they are about to meet. As you read, answer the questions. They will help you to develop your understanding of this text.

The story so far...

Artemis Fowl (aged twelve, Irish, criminal mastermind) is travelling with his trusty sidekick and bodyguard, Butler, in Vietnam. Butler is armed with weapons and technology to help them in their mission. They are tracking down 'the Book', which contains Fairy secrets, as part of Artemis's plan to restore his family's fortune. A secret contact has been in touch with information about where a healer who might be able to help hides herself. The contact leads Artemis and Butler along steaming alleyways to the shadows where she is hiding...

The two worlds meet

Butler plucked a set of night-vision glasses from his belt and placed them in Artemis's outstretched hand. The focus motor buzzed to suit the light.

Artemis fixed the glasses to his face. Everything became radioactive green. Taking a deep breath, he turned his gaze to the squirming shadows. Something
5 squatted on a raffia mat, shifting uneasily in the almost non-existent light. Artemis fine-tuned the focus. The figure was small, abnormally so, and wrapped in a filthy shawl. Empty spirit jugs were half-buried in the mud around her. One forearm poked from the material. It seemed green. But then, so did everything else.

'Madam,' he said, 'I have a proposition for you.'
10 The figure's head wobbled sleepily.

'Wine,' she rasped, her voice like nails on a school board. 'Wine, English.'

Artemis smiled. **The gift of tongues**, aversion to light. Check, check.

'Irish, actually. Now, about my proposition?'

The healer shook a bony finger craftily. 'Wine first. Then talk.'
15 'Butler?'

The bodyguard reached into a pocket and drew out a half-pint of the finest Irish whiskey. Artemis took the bottle and held it teasingly beyond the shadows. He barely had time to remove his goggles when the claw-like hand darted from the gloom to snatch the whiskey. A mottled green hand.
20 There was no doubt.

Artemis swallowed a triumphant grin.

'Now, madam, you have something that I want.'

The healer's tongue caught a drop of alcohol at the corner of her mouth.
25 'Yes, Irish. Sore head. Bad tooth. I heal.'

1 Whose eyes does the reader see through?

2 What are your first impressions of the figure in the shadows?

3 What are the differences between the ways Artemis speaks and the ways the 'healer' speaks?

Word bank

the gift of tongues
the ability to speak many languages

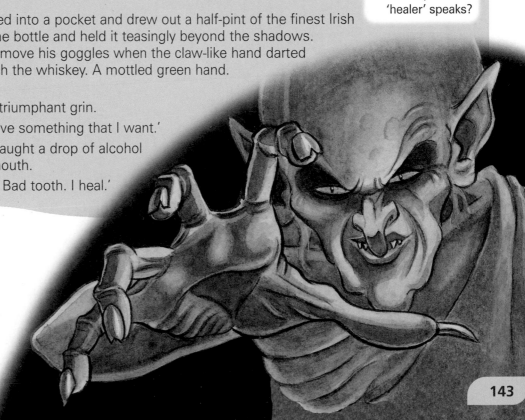

143

Artemis replaced the night-vision goggles and squatted to her level. 'I am perfectly healthy, madam, apart from a slight dust-mite allergy, and I don't think even you can do anything about that. No. What I want from you is your Book.'

The hag froze. Bright eyes glinted from beneath the shawl.

30 'Book?' she said cautiously. 'I don't know about no book. I am healer. You want book, go to library.' Artemis sighed with exaggerated patience. 'You are no healer. You are a **sprite**, **p'shog**, fairy, **ka-dalun**. Whichever language you prefer to use. And I want your Book.'

For a long moment the creature said nothing, then she threw back the shawl
35 from her forehead. In the green glow of the night-vision goggles, her features leaped at Artemis like a Hallowe'en mask. The fairy's nose was long and hooked under two slitted golden eyes. Her ears were pointed, and the alcohol addiction had melted her skin like putty.

> **Word bank**
>
> **sprite, p'shog, ka-dalun** different names for fairies

4 What do you learn about the Book from the reactions of the 'healer'?

5 What do you think is the importance of the goggles to:
a Artemis
b the way the reader is shown things?

Use of similes

When a writer creates an image in readers' minds by comparing one thing to something else, we call it a simile. In a simile you often see the words *as* or *like*.

Activity 3

1 Re-read the following similes and answer the questions.

> 'Wine,' she rasped, <u>her voice like nails on a school board</u>.

a What kind of noise do nails make on a school board?
b What does this tell you about the sound of the fairy's voice?

> He barely had time to remove his goggles when the <u>claw-like hand</u> darted from the gloom to snatch the whiskey.

c What is a claw like?
d What does this suggest about the appearance of the fairy's hand?

2 Create your own similes to describe different kinds of voices. You can make up your own sentence starters or use these.
a 'I feel sick,' the girl croaked like …
b 'Pass it here,' the player ordered like …
c 'Don't make any noise,' the boy whispered like …
d 'Goal!' the crowd screamed like …

Feedback

1 In groups of four, talk about what makes a good simile. Write three rules for what a good simile should do.

2 Read the similes you have written. Choose the best one for **2a**, **b**, **c** and **d**. Write a short explanation of the reasons for each choice. Present your choices and your reasons to another group of four or to the whole class.

Use of verbs and adverbs

A verb is a word that expresses an action, a happening, a process or a state. It is sometimes called a 'doing' or 'being' word. The writer of *Artemis Fowl* chooses his verbs carefully to create particular effects.

> Butler plucked a set of night-vision glasses from his belt and placed them in Artemis's outstretched hand. (page 143, lines 1–2)

The verbs 'plucked' and 'placed' both tell the reader something about Butler. They suggest that he is very careful and precise in what he does. They suggest he is not the kind of person to make a mistake.

Activity 4

1 Write down what you learn from the verbs 'froze' and 'glinted' in the following lines.

> ' … No. What I want from you is your Book.'
>   The hag froze. Bright eyes glinted from beneath the shawl.
> (page 144, lines 28–9)

2 Sometimes the writer uses adverbs to give extra meaning to a verb.
   a What is suggested by the adverb in each of these sentences?

   b Explore the difference adverbs can make by swapping the adverbs in the two sentences. How are the meanings of the sentences changed?

3 Scan page 143 lines 16–20 to find another example of the use of an adverb.
  a Copy the sentence that contains the adverb and underline the adverb.
  b Note down what the adverb shows you about Artemis.
  c List other adverbs that could have been used in its place. For each one, compare it with the one actually used. What difference would it make?

Use of adjectives

Adjectives are words that describe somebody or something.
Adjectives can come before a noun – for example:

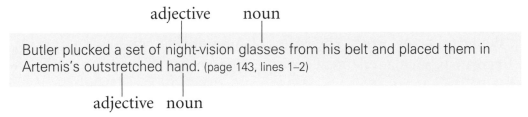

adjective   noun

Butler plucked a set of night-vision glasses from his belt and placed them in Artemis's outstretched hand. (page 143, lines 1–2)

adjective   noun

Adjectives can come after verbs such as *become, get, seem, look, be* – for example:

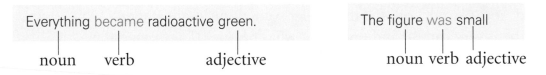

Everything became radioactive green.

noun   verb   adjective

The figure was small

noun verb adjective

Activity 5

1 Copy the following sentences.
  a Underline the adjectives in them.
  b Say what each adjective suggests to you.

> The figure shook a bony finger craftily.

> A mottled green hand.

2 With a partner, try to think of other adjectives you could use in these two sentences to create a different meaning.

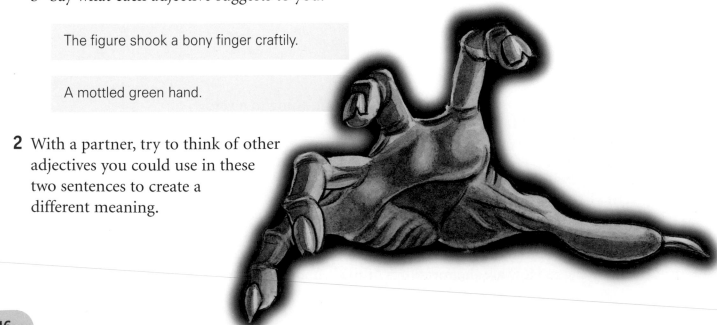

Progress check

1 To check you understand how writers use similes, verbs and adjectives, copy the following paragraph and underline or highlight:
   - two similes
   - at least four verbs
   - at least four adjectives.

> For a long moment the creature said nothing, then she threw back the shawl from her forehead. In the green glow of the night-vision goggles, her features leaped at Artemis like a Hallowe'en mask. The fairy's nose was long and hooked under two slitted golden eyes. Her ears were pointed, and the alcohol addiction had melted her skin like putty.
> (page 144, lines 34–8)

2 To check your awareness of the effect of these features, copy and complete the following sentences.
   a *Eoin Colfer uses the simile* _____ (choose your simile and quote it) *to suggest* _____ (explain the effects of the simile).
   b *The adjectives used to describe the fairy's nose and eyes are* _____ (list them). *They make her seem* _____ (explain the effects of the adjectives).

3 Imagine a very beautiful fairy or a very ugly monster. Write a paragraph in which you describe the creature. In your description you should aim to use:
   - two similes
   - at least four verbs
   - at least four adjectives.

4 When you have written your description, ask a partner to check it for you. They should underline each of the ten features you were asked to use and give you one mark for each. If you get less than seven marks, you need to add to your description.

Character and setting

You have seen how a writer uses genre, similes, verbs, adverbs and adjectives to create vivid descriptions. You are now going to investigate further how a writer builds character and setting.

Character

Writers use different ways to reveal their characters and help us to understand them. They describe how characters look and tell you about their characteristics. They also reveal characters by showing you the way they think, speak and behave.

Readers often bring their own knowledge and expectations about different *kinds* of characters to what they read. The writer can build on this, or surprise the reader by making a character different from what they expected.

Activity 6

To help you explore how a central character is revealed in *Artemis Fowl*, talk about the fairies you know of in other stories. Keep notes of your discussion.

- Is there a traditional good fairy?
- Is there a traditional bad fairy?
- What do they look like?
- How do they behave?
- What connection do they have with humans?
- Can you think of any other kinds of fairies? What are they like?

Now read on. Answer the questions as you read.

The story so far...

The hag we meet early on in *Artemis Fowl* is from a group of fairies who have been led astray by evils in the world of man. Artemis manages to borrow 'the Book' of fairy secrets from her, photographs it, transfers it to his computer and heads home to Dublin. Artemis needs the fairy secrets to get their gold. He wants the gold to restore his family name because his father lost the family fortune in Russia and never returned. Artemis cleverly cracks the fairy code the book is written in and starts to plot what he does best – dastardly acts. As Artemis does this, the reader is introduced to another central character in the book.

Holly

Holly Short was lying in bed having a silent fume. Nothing unusual about this. Leprechauns in general were not known for their geniality. But Holly was in an exceptionally bad mood, even for a fairy. Technically she was an elf, fairy being a general term. She was a leprechaun too, but that was just a job.

5 Perhaps a description would be more helpful than a lecture on fairy genealogy. Holly Short had nut-brown skin, cropped auburn hair and hazel eyes. Her nose had a hook and her mouth was plump and cherubic, which was
10 appropriate considering that Cupid was her great-grandfather. Her mother was a European elf with a fiery temper and a willowy figure. Holly, too, had a slim frame, with long
15 tapered fingers perfect for wrapping around a buzz baton. Her ears, of course, were pointed. At exactly one metre in height, Holly was only a centimetre below the fairy average, but
20 even one centimetre can make an awful lot of difference when you don't have many to spare.

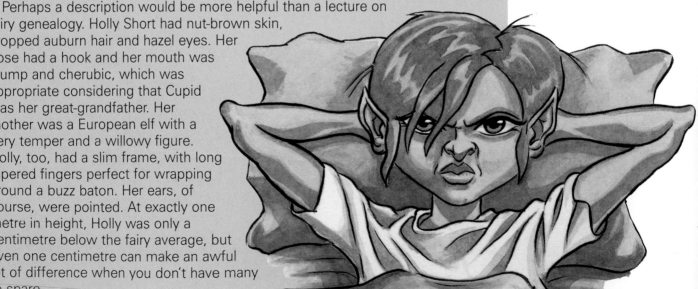

1 Think back to your conversation about the traditional picture of fairies. How does the description of Holly match with this picture?

2 In lines 5–22 the writer gives us a physical description of Holly, which is one way of describing a character. List the details he gives. What do the details tell you about Holly?

3 List details of the physical appearance of a person you know well. It could be a parent, a brother, a sister or a friend. Ask a partner what extra details are needed to help them imagine what this person looks like. Add these to your list.

4 Characteristics are a character's distinguishing qualities. The writer reveals Holly's characteristics by telling us things about her. In line 26 below we discover Holly is brave, as she has chosen a dangerous job. Find evidence in these lines that suggests she is also:
   a determined   b irresponsible.

Characteristics	Evidence
brave	Holly has chosen a dangerous job.
determined	
irresponsible	

Commander Root was the cause of Holly's distress. Root had been on Holly's case since day one. The commander had decided to take offence at the fact
25 that the first female officer in **Recon's** history had been assigned to his squad. Recon was a notoriously dangerous posting with a high fatality rate, and Root didn't think it was any place for a girlie. Well, he was just going to have to get used to the idea, because Holly Short had no intention of quitting for him or anybody else.
30   Though she'd never admit it, another possible cause for Holly's irritability was the **Ritual**. She'd been meaning to perform it for several moons now, but somehow there just never seemed to be time. And if Root found out she was running low on magic, she'd be transferred to Traffic for sure.

> **Word bank**
>
> **Recon** elite branch of the police
> **Ritual** fairy ceremony to top-up magic

5 Another way of revealing character is by getting inside a character's head and showing their thoughts. From reading lines 34–64 below, what do you learn of what Holly thinks about:
   a humans   b working underground   c goblins?

Holly rolled off her futon and stumbled into the shower. That was one
35 advantage of living near the earth's core – the water was always hot. No natural
light, of course, but that was a small price to pay for privacy Underground. The
last human-free zone. There was nothing like coming home after a long day on
the job, switching off your shield and sinking into a bubbling slime pool. Bliss.

The fairy suited up, zipping the dull-green jumpsuit up to her chin and
40 strapping on her helmet. LEPrecon uniforms were smart these days. Not like
that top-o'-the-morning costume the force had had to wear back in the old
days. Buckled shoes and knickerbockers! Honestly. No wonder leprechauns
were such ridiculous figures in human folklore. Still, probably better that way. If
the Mud People knew that the word 'leprechaun' actually originated from
45 LEPrecon, an elite branch of Lower Elements Police, they'd probably take steps
to stamp them out. Better to stay inconspicuous and let the humans have their
stereotypes.

With the moon already rising on the surface, there was no time for a proper
breakfast. Holly grabbed the remains of a nettle smoothie from the cooler and
50 drank it in the tunnels. As usual there was chaos in the main thoroughfare.
Airborne sprites jammed the avenue like stones in a bottle. The gnomes weren't
helping either, lumbering along with their big swinging behinds blocking two
lanes. Swear toads infested every damp patch, cursing like sailors. That
particular breed began as a joke but had multiplied into an epidemic. Someone
55 lost their wand over that one.

Holly battled through the crowds to the police station. There was already a
riot outside Spud's Spud **Emporium**. LEP Corporal Newt was trying to sort it
out. Good luck to him. Nightmare. At least Holly got the chance to work
above ground.

60 The LEP station doors were crammed with protesters. The goblin/dwarf **turf
war** had flared up again, and every morning hordes of angry parents showed up
demanding the release of their innocent offspring. Holly snorted. If there actually
was an innocent goblin, Holly Short had yet to meet him. They were clogging up
the cells now, howling gang chants and hurling fireballs at each other.

> 6 A different way of revealing a character is through the way they
>   behave and talk. What do you learn about Holly in lines 65–93
>   below from:
>   a   the things she does   b   the things she says?

65   Holly shouldered her way into the throng. 'Coming through,' she grunted.
'Police business.'

They were on her like flies on a stink-worm.

'My Grumpo is innocent!'

'Police brutality!'

70 'Officer, could you take my baby in his blanky? He can't sleep without it.'

Holly set her visor to reflect and ignored them all. Once upon a time the uniform would have earned you some respect. Not any more. Now you were a target. 'Excuse me, Officer, but I seem to have misplaced my jar of warts.' 'Pardon me, young elf, but my cat's climbed a stalactite.' Or, 'If you have a
75 minute, Captain, could you tell me how to get to the Fountain of Youth?' Holly shuddered. Tourists. She had troubles of her own. More than she knew, as she was about to find out.

In the station lobby, a **kleptomaniac** dwarf was busy picking the pockets of everyone else in the booking line, including the officer he was handcuffed to.
80 Holly gave him a swipe in the backside with her buzz baton. The electric charge singed the seat of his leather trousers.

'Whatcha doing there, Mulch?'

Mulch started, **contraband** dropping from his sleeves.

'Officer Short,' he whined, his face a mask of regret, 'I can't help myself. It's
85 my nature.'

'I know that, Mulch. And it's our nature to throw you in a cell for a couple of centuries.'

She winked at the dwarf's arresting officer.

'Nice to see you're staying alert.'

90 The elf blushed, kneeling to pick up his wallet and badge.

Holly forged past Root's office, hoping she would make it to the cubicle before …

'SHORT! GET IN HERE!'

Word bank

Emporium a shop that sells a range of goods
turf war a fight over a piece of land
kleptomaniac someone who can't resist stealing
contraband forbidden, smuggled or stolen goods

As you have seen, a writer can reveal a character to the reader by:

- giving a physical description
- telling the reader about distinguishing qualities or characteristics
- showing the character's thoughts
- showing the way the character behaves
- showing the way the character speaks.

 Highlight thinking

Using observation

It is helpful to use what you observe to shape your thoughts and decisions.

Here in Activity 7 you are using what you have observed about the world of *Artemis Fowl* to create a character that fits in. You are also organising, comparing and discussing your observations in order to create something new.

Think about where else you might use these skills.

Activity 7

Copy and complete the following planning frame to help you plan the details of a character that would fit into the world of fairies in *Artemis Fowl*.

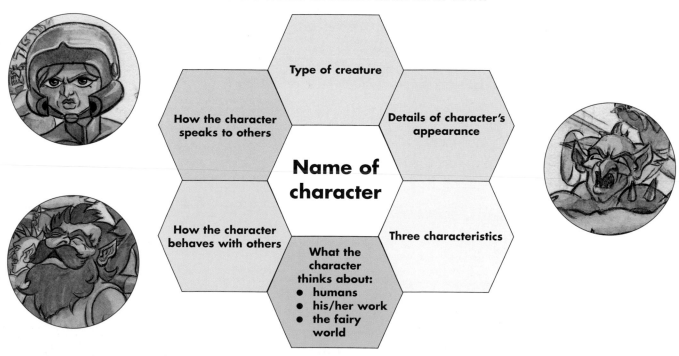

Feedback

Portrait artists need to capture a person's character as well as what they look like.

1 Imagine you are a portrait artist. You have been asked to draw a particular creature. To do this well, you need to have a clear idea of the creature's appearance and character.
   a Look at either your own notes or a partner's. Is there enough detail to:
      - show what the creature looks like
      - capture the creature's personality?
   b If not, what other detail do you need? Either add the necessary detail to your own notes or tell your partner what is missing from their notes.

Setting

You have explored a range of techniques that writers use to introduce and establish characters. As writers introduce characters, so they also introduce a sense of place. The place where the action of a story occurs is the setting.

In Chapter 1 the writer sets the scene for the story by bringing together Artemis and the fairy world (see the text on pages 143–4).
In Chapter 3 he gives more detail about what the fairy world itself is like (see the text on pages 148–51).

Activity 8

1 With a partner, scan the text on pages 150–1 to find details about the setting. Make notes under the following sub-headings.
  - What the place is like.
  - The kinds of things that happen there.
  - The kinds of creatures who live there.

2 Look at the details you have selected. Choose three words from the list below that you think best describe this place. For each word you choose, give at least one reason, based on your notes, that explains your choice.

chaotic   magical   unpleasant   mysterious   funny   dangerous

Narrative techniques

You are going to explore how a writer uses different narrative techniques when telling a story. First, remind yourself of the meaning of the following terms:
  - narrate – to tell a story
  - narrative – the story itself
  - narration – the act of telling a story
  - narrator – the person telling the story

Narrative perspective

Narrative perspective is the point of view from which a writer chooses to tell a story. In *Artemis Fowl* the story is told from the point of view of someone outside the story. This is called the third person. Characters are referred to by name or as *he*, *she* (third person singular) or *they* (third person plural) – for example:

> She could do the tourist thing all night once her business was complete.
> (page 154, lines 13–14)
> They crept into the night with practised silence. (page 155, line 28)

Using narrative techniques

You are going to continue reading from *Artemis Fowl*, and explore the writer's use of the third person.

The story so far…

Holly, the first 'girl' fairy that Commander Root has let work in Recon squad as a 'test case', is in trouble. Again. She's just messed up her most recent case and Root tells her she's back on Traffic. Holly is angry. What about all her successes? As she argues, the phone goes. A crisis. A rogue troll is on the loose. Holly offers to help, and Root is desperate. He gives her one more chance. But Holly is running low on magic. She's neglected to do 'the ritual' to top it up. Her magic runs out while chasing the troll, resulting in chaos. Somehow, Holly rescues the situation. When Root finds her he commands her to 'get out of here and don't come back until you're full to the tips of your ears with magic'. Meanwhile, Artemis has cracked the fairy code of 'the Book' to get the fairy gold. He's read about the fairy ritual, and is lying in wait with his bodyguard Butler to take a fairy captive while performing the ritual.

Abduction

1   In using the third person, the writer cleverly shows us what the characters are thinking by getting inside their heads and capturing their thoughts. Examples of this are highlighted in the first paragraph. Identify and copy, or talk about, other examples of Holly's thoughts being put into words in the rest of the passage.

Holly hooked the wings over a low branch, unstrapping the helmet to give her ears some air. You had to be careful with elfin ears – a few hours in the helmet and they started to flake. She gave the tips a massage. No dry skin there. That was because she had a daily moisturising regime, not like some
5   of the male LEP officers. When they took off their helmets, you'd swear it had just started to snow.

Holly paused for a minute to admire the view. Ireland certainly was picturesque. Even the Mud People hadn't been able to destroy that. Not yet anyway … Give them another century or two. The river was folding
10   gently before her like a silver snake, hissing as the water tumbled across a stony bed. The oak tree crackled overhead, its branches rasping together in the bracing breeze.

Now, to work. She could do the tourist thing all night once her business was complete. A seed. She needed a seed. Holly bent to the
15   ground, brushing the dried leaves and twigs from the clay's surface. Her fingers closed around a smooth acorn. That wasn't hard now, was it? she thought. All that remained for her to do was plant it somewhere else and her powers would come rushing back.

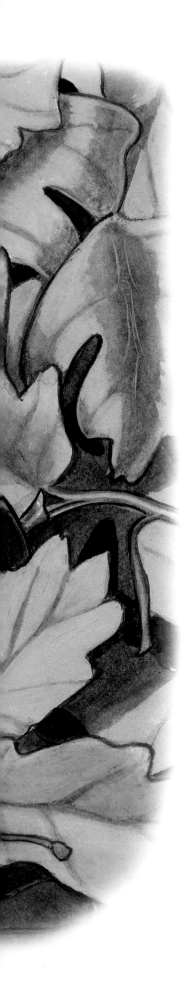

2　One advantage of writing in the third person is that it allows the writer:
- to shift the focus from one person or place to another
- to know extra things.

   a　What shift takes place in the focus between lines 1–18 and 19?
   b　What extra information does the writer give about Butler's gun?

20 Butler checked the porta-radar, muting the volume in case the equipment betrayed their position. The red arm swept the screen with agonising lethargy, and then … *Flash!* An upright figure by the tree. Too small for an adult, the wrong proportions for a child. He gave Artemis the thumbs-up. Possible match.

    Artemis nodded, strapping the mirrored sunglasses across his brow. Butler followed his lead, popping the cap on his weapon's starlight scope. This was no
25 ordinary dart rifle. It had been specially tooled for a Kenyan ivory hunter and had the range and rapid-fire capacity of a Kalashnikov. Butler had picked it up for a song from the government official after the ivory poacher's execution.

3　Think about lines 28–42 below. In what ways would they be different if it was Artemis telling the story, or Holly telling the story? Imagine you are either Artemis or Holly telling the story.
   Talk about:
- what you could know
- what you couldn't know.

They crept into the night with practised silence. The diminutive figure before them unhooked a contraption from around its shoulders and lifted a full-face helmet
30 from a definitely non-human head. Butler wrapped the rifle strap twice round his wrist, pulling the stock into his shoulder. He activated the scope and a red dot appeared in the centre of the figure's back. Artemis nodded and his manservant squeezed the trigger.

    In spite of a million to one odds, it was at that precise moment that the figure
35 bent low to the earth.

    Something whizzed over Holly's head, something that glinted in the starlight. Holly had enough on-the-job experience to realise that she was under fire, and immediately curled her elfin frame into a ball, minimising the target.

    She drew her pistol, rolling towards the shelter of the tree trunk. Her brain
40 scrambled for possibilities. Who could be shooting at her and why?

    Something was waiting beside the tree. Something roughly the size of a mountain, but considerably more mobile.

4　The use of **dialogue** is also an important narrative technique. It can:
- allow information to be passed from one character to another
- allow the reader to find out important things about characters
- help to make characters and situations more interesting.

Read lines 45–82 below, then answer these questions.
  a Why is Holly surprised that Artemis calls her 'fairy'?
  b What does Holly say to try to frighten Artemis?
  c What different things does Holly discover that Artemis knows?
  d What do you find out about the kind of person Artemis is by
     the way he talks to Holly?

'Nice pea-shooter,' grinned the figure, smothering Holly's gun hand in
a turnip-sized fist.

45 Holly managed to extricate her fingers in a nanosecond before
they snapped like brittle spaghetti.

'I don't suppose you would consider peaceful surrender?' said a
cold voice behind her.

Holly turned, elbows raised for combat.

50 'No,' sighed the boy melodramatically. 'I suppose not.'

Holly put on her best brave face.

'Stay back, human. You don't know what you're dealing with.'

The boy laughed. 'I believe, fairy, that you are the one unfamiliar with
the facts.'

55 Fairy? He knew she was a fairy.

'I have magic, mud-worm. Enough to turn you and your
gorilla into pig droppings.'

The boy took a step closer. 'Brave words, miss. But lies
nonetheless. If, as you say, you had magic, you would have
60 no doubt used it by now. No, I suspect that you have gone too
long without the Ritual and you are here to replenish your powers.'

Holly was dumbfounded. There was a human before her, casually spouting
sacred secrets. This was disastrous. Catastrophic. It could mean the end of
generations of peace. If the humans were aware of a fairy subculture, it was only
65 a matter of time before the two species went to war. She must do something,
and there was only one weapon left in her arsenal.

The mesmer is the lowest form of magic and requires only a trickle of power.
There are even certain humans with a bent for the talent. It is within the ability of
even the most drained fairy to put a complete mind **kibosh** on any human alive.

70 Holly summoned the final dribble of magic from the base of her skull.

'Human,' she intoned, her voice suddenly resonating with bass tones, 'your will
is mine.'

Artemis smiled, safe behind his mirrored lenses. 'I doubt it,' he said, and
nodded curtly.

75 Holly felt the dart puncture the suit's toughened material, depositing its load of
curare and succinylcholine chloride-based **tranquilliser** into her shoulder. The
world instantly dissolved into a series of technicoloured bubbles and, try as she
might, Holly couldn't seem to hold on to more than one thought. And that thought
was: how did they know? It spiralled around her head as she sank into
80 unconsciousness. How did they know? How did they know? How did they …

Mixing dialogue with narrative detail

A story with just dialogue, or too much dialogue, can be boring. By mixing dialogue with narrative detail writers can paint a very clear picture for the reader. In the following lines the dialogue and narrative detail are shown in different colours. The annotations explain the effects of the words.

Sharpen punctuation

Three-dot ellipsis (…)
Ellipsis is used twice in the text. The first time is in lines 8–9: 'Not yet anyway …'

1 Read what comes before and after line 8–9. What is the writer suggesting by this use of ellipsis?
2 Find one other example of the use of ellipsis in the text. Copy it out and give the line number. Write one sentence explaining what the writer is suggesting by this use of ellipsis.
3 Use what you have discovered to write one rule for when to use ellipsis.

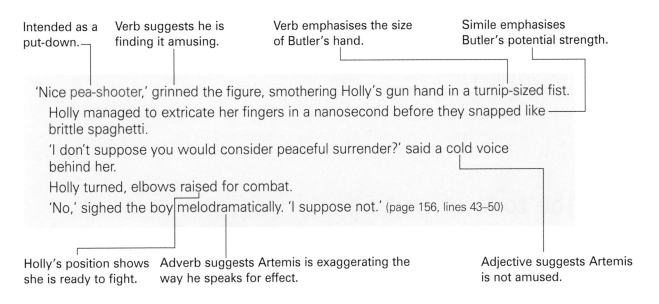

Intended as a put-down.

Verb suggests he is finding it amusing.

Verb emphasises the size of Butler's hand.

Simile emphasises Butler's potential strength.

'Nice pea-shooter,' grinned the figure, smothering Holly's gun hand in a turnip-sized fist.
Holly managed to extricate her fingers in a nanosecond before they snapped like brittle spaghetti.
'I don't suppose you would consider peaceful surrender?' said a cold voice behind her.
Holly turned, elbows raised for combat.
'No,' sighed the boy melodramatically. 'I suppose not.' (page 156, lines 43–50)

Holly's position shows she is ready to fight.

Adverb suggests Artemis is exaggerating the way he speaks for effect.

Adjective suggests Artemis is not amused.

Activity 9

1 a Copy the following lines. Highlight the dialogue in one colour. Highlight the narrative detail in a different colour.

  b Write your own annotations for the words that are underlined to show why the writer has used them.

> Holly <u>put on</u> her best brave face.
> 'Stay back, human. You don't know what you're dealing with.'
> The boy <u>laughed</u>. 'I believe, fairy, that you are the one unfamiliar with the facts.'
> <u>Fairy?</u> He knew she was a fairy.
> 'I have magic, <u>mud-worm</u>. Enough to turn you and <u>your gorilla</u> into <u>pig droppings</u>.'
> <u>The boy</u> took a step closer. 'Brave words, <u>miss</u>. But lies nonetheless…'
> (page 156, lines 51–9)

2 Think ahead to when Holly wakes from unconsciousness. She is very angry to have been captured and the boy is amused by her anger. Write about six lines of dialogue and narrative detail to show what they say to each other and how they say it.

✓ Progress check

1 Look back over what you have studied so far in this unit. Write a short advice leaflet for Year 5 pupils on *either*:
- different ways to make your characters come alive, *or*
- clever narrative techniques.

Your advice leaflet should:
- be no more than one side in length
- be set out with headings and sub-headings
- give clear advice in a simple way.

Include all the main points but do not copy directly from the book. Year 5 students might not understand it.

2 When you have finished, ask a partner to read your leaflet and check your headings against what has been covered in this unit on pages 147–52 or 153–8.

Exploring the tone of writing

Writers make choices about how they tell a story. The choices create a tone. For example, a story about a rowdy lesson in school could have several different tones: it could be funny, angry or serious.

Creating tone

You are going to explore some of the techniques used by the writer of *Artemis Fowl* to create the tone of the story. This will help you to understand the techniques and to learn how to use them in your own writing.

Activity 10

As you read the following extract on page 159–60, decide whether the tone the writer has used is:

a largely serious, or

b generally humorous.

Give at least two reasons for your choice.

The story so far...
Artemis has worked out from the fairy book he's stolen that there's a fairy hostage fund, and it's the best way to get hold of fairy gold. So Artemis captures fairy Holly when she is low on magic and has started the ritual to top it up, taking her hostage at his home. Holly is angry at being caught. Then she realises she has the acorn she picked up as part of her ritual to get her magic back. All she needs is some earth and her powers will be restored. Meanwhile, Artemis and his bodyguard Butler lie in wait for Commander Root and the fairy commandos, who will try to rescue Holly. But as the fairy commandos approach Fowl Manor, they don't realise they are being watched...

Retrieval commandos

LEPretrieval One were the best and the brightest. It was every little fairy's dream that one day he would grow up to don the stealth-black jumpsuit of the Retrieval commandos. These were the elite. Trouble was their middle name. In the case of Captain Kelp, Trouble was actually his first name. He'd insisted on it
5 at his manhood ceremony, having just been accepted into the Academy.

Trouble led his team down the sweeping avenue. As usual, he took the point position himself, determined to be the first into the fray if, as he fervently hoped, a fray developed.

'Check in,' he whispered into the mike that wound snake-like from his helmet.
10 'Negative on one.'

'Nothing, Captain.'

'A big negatori, Trouble.'

Captain Kelp winced.

'We're in the field, Corporal. Follow procedure.'
15 'But Mummy said!'

'I don't care what Mummy said, Corporal! Rank is rank! You will refer to me as Captain Kelp.'

'Yessir, Captain,' sulked the corporal. 'But don't ask me to iron your tunic any more.'

20 Trouble zeroed in on his brother's channel, shutting out the rest of the squad.

'Shut up about Mummy, will you? And the ironing. You're only on this mission because I requested you! Now start
25 acting like a professional or get back to the perimeter!'

'OK, Trubs.'

'Trouble!' shouted Captain Kelp. 'It's Trouble. Not Trubs, or Trub. Trouble! OK?'
30 'OK. *Trouble*. Mummy's right. You're only a baby.'

Swearing very unprofessionally, Captain Kelp switched his headset back to the open channel. He was just in time to hear an unusual sound.

35   *'Arrkk.'*

      'What was that?'

      'What?'

      'Dunno.'

      'Nothing, Captain.'

40   But Trouble had done a Sound Recognition in-service for his captain's exam, and he was pretty sure the *'Arrkk'* had been caused by someone getting a chop across the windpipe. More than likely his brother had walked into a shrub.

      'Grub? Are you all right?'

      'That's Corporal Grub to you.'

45   Kelp viciously kicked a daisy.

      'Check in. Sound off in sequence.'

      'One, OK.'

      'Two, fine.'

      'Three, bored but alive.'

50   'Five approaching west wing.'

      Kelp froze. 'Wait. Four? You there, Four? What's your situation?'

      '.....................' Nothing except static.

      'Right, Four is down. Possibly an equipment malfunction. Still, we can't afford to take any chances. Regroup by the main door.'

55   Retrieval One crept together, making slightly less noise than a silk spider. Kelp did a quick head count. Eleven. One short of a full complement. Four was probably wandering around the rose bushes, wondering why nobody was talking to him.

      Then Trouble noticed two things – one, a pair of black boots was sticking out

60 of a shrub beside the door, and two, there was a massive human standing in the doorway. The figure was cradling a very nasty-looking gun in the crook of his arm.

Using character names to create tone

Writers often invent names for the characters in their stories. When you are thinking about the tone of a piece of writing, it helps to look at the names writers have chosen. These names can contribute to the 'tone' of the story.

Activity 11

1 'Kelp' and 'Grub' are the names of two characters in the text you read on pages 159–60. Use a dictionary to check the meanings of these words. Then explain why a reader might find them funny.

2 Below is a short piece of writing with a fairly serious tone. Imagine the police have heard about strange activities at Fowl Manor and call by later to find out what's happening. Make the tone more humorous by changing the

underlined names. Use 'real' words that can be found in the dictionary rather than nonsense words.

> Master <u>Windsor</u> opened the door. The butler, <u>Smythe</u>, was standing there, a card in his gloved hand. 'There are two police officers at the door, Sir: Chief Inspector <u>Sutcliffe</u> and Sergeant <u>Wilson</u>.'

3 In the first half of the text on page 159, the writer plays with the name 'Trouble'. Captain Kelp chose the name 'Trouble' because he enjoys danger and because anyone who bothers him will be in trouble. With this in mind, re-read lines 27–31:

> 'OK, Trubs.'
>   'Trouble!' shouted Captain Kelp. 'It's Trouble. Not Trubs, or Trub. Trouble! OK?'
>   'OK. *Trouble*. Mummy's right. You're only a baby.'

a   How has the writer used the character's name to create a humorous tone?

b   What should these characters be talking about instead of their names?

c   What do you think is the difference between using the name 'Trubs' and 'Trouble'?

d   Kelp likes to think he's in charge. How does the dialogue above show he's having problems controlling his troops?

Using language to create tone

Writers also create tone by their choice of words and language such as alliteration, onomatopoeia and comparison.

Activity 12

> **Alliteration** is the repeated use of the same sound at the start of words that are quite close together. It can also be used to create a humorous tone.

1 Read the sentence below aloud, which emphasises the letter 'f'. Does it make Kelp seem a little ridiculous? How?

> As usual, he took the point position himself, determined to be the first into the fray if, as he fervently hoped, a fray developed. (page 159, lines 6–8)

2 Look at this serious sentence: *Fearlessly he flew into the battle.*
  a Re-write this sentence adding words to create more humour by exaggerating *either*:
- the use of words beginning with 'f', *or*
- the use of words beginning with 'b'.

  b Read your finished sentence aloud, emphasising the letter you repeated.

> **Onomatopoeia** is the use of words that sound like the thing they describe, for example: *thwack, moo, crash* or *hiss.*

Activity 13

1 In the text on page 160, line 35, the writer uses 'Arrkk' to describe the sound of 'someone getting a chop across the windpipe'. How does the spelling of 'Arrkk' suggest the writer's humorous intentions?

2 Copy out lines 35–42 from the text on page 160. Keeping the same humorous tone as the original, replace:
  a 'Arrkk' with a different made-up sound
  b 'someone getting a chop across the windpipe' with your own idea of what your new word sounds like.

> **Comic comparisons** are another technique that writers use to create a humorous tone, by making exaggerated or absurd links between one thing and another.

Activity 14

1 Look again at this comparison from the text on page 160, line 55. In what way is it exaggerated and/or absurd?

> Retrieval One crept together, making slightly less noise than a silk spider.

2 Write out the sentence below. Make up your own absurd comparison to end it.

Retrieval One crept together, making slightly less noise than _____.

Bringing narrative techniques together

You have explored a range of techniques used by the writer of *Artemis Fowl* to create a humorous tone:
- the use of names
- alliteration
- onomatopoeia
- comparison.

Activity 15

To show your understanding of these techniques, create a scene of your own using as many of them as you can. You should write just one paragraph, not a complete story.

Use these guidelines to help you.

- Think of a similar dangerous situation – some people sneaking up on someone else. Include three characters – two sneaking up and one waiting.
- Think of names that do not suit this situation. Try to use these names to create humour.
- Use alliteration, onomatopoeia and similes in your situation.

Feedback

1 When you have finished, swap your piece of writing with a partner. Give each other feedback on how well you created a humorous tone.
   - Did your partner's writing make you smile?
   - Did they play with names and the sound of words effectively?
   - Did they use alliteration and similes in ways that created a humorous tone?

2 Think about your partner's feedback on your writing and make any improvements.

Creating suspense

You have seen how a writer creates tone. You are now going to look at how a writer creates suspense. With a partner, discuss what you think 'suspense' means. Can you think of examples from books, films or television that would help someone to understand what suspense is? Why do you think readers or viewers like suspense?

Building suspense

Read the text on pages 164–5. You may have come across similar scenes in thriller stories. This kind of scene is usually very tense and exciting, filled with suspense. As you read, the questions around the text will help you to focus on the techniques the writer uses to build suspense. Compare your answers with a partner.

> The story so far...
> Artemis has captured fairy Holly to hold her ransom in exchange for gold. Commander Root has led a Retrieval Squad to rescue her but they've failed. Artemis knows too much about fairy magic for the attack to succeed, because he's read the stolen copy of 'the Book' containing fairy secrets. So the commander has to negotiate with Artemis, who asks for one tonne of 24-carat gold. But the fairies don't want to give up their gold. So to get Holly back, they need to 'bend' fairy rules and do something that Artemis won't expect. They send for Mulch, an earth-eating, criminal dwarf. Although he's a convict and thief, they release him from prison and he tunnels under Fowl Manor, to the rescue. He eats through, but the earth plays havoc with his insides. Mulch is in radio contact with Commander Julius Root and Foaly (their technical expert) who has led Mulch to a safe...

Breaking the safe

Mulch squinted at the safe. It was incredible. He could see right into the works. Tumblers and catches stood out in the shadowy relief. He blew on his hairy fingers and twisted the combination dial. In seconds the safe lay open before him.

5 'Oh,' he said, disappointed.

'What is it?

'Nothing. Just human currency. Nothing of value.'

'Leave it,' ordered Root. 'Try another room. Get going.'

Mulch nodded. Another room. Before his time ran out. But something was
10 niggling at him. If this guy was so clever, why did he put the safe behind a painting? Such a cliché. Totally against form. No. Something wasn't right here. They were being duped somehow.

Mulch closed the safe, swinging the portrait back into position. It swung smoothly, weightless on the hinges. Weightless. He swung the pictures out
15 again. And back in.

'Convict. What are you doing?'

'Shut up, Julius! I mean, quiet a moment, Commander.'

Mulch squinted at the frame's profile. A bit thicker than normal. Quite a bit thicker. Even taking the box frame into account. Five centimetres. He ran a nail
20 down the heavy cartridge backing and stripped it away to reveal …

'Another safe.'

A smaller one. Custom-made, obviously.

'Foaly, I can't see through this.'

'Lead-lined. You're on you own, burglar boy. Do what you do best.'

25 'Typical,' muttered Mulch, flattening his ear to the cold steel.

He twirled the dial experimentally. Nice action. The clicks were muted by the lead, he would have to concentrate. The upside was that something this thin could have only three **tumblers** at the most.

> 1 How do 'something' and 'somehow' help the writer to create suspense?

> 2 Root is not in the room with Mulch. These 'interruptions' slow the action down. Why might the writer have included them?

> **Word bank**
>
> **tumblers** the parts of a lock that move when you turn the key

Mulch held his breath and twisted the dial, one cog at a time. To the normal
30 ear, even with amplification, the clicks would have seemed uniform. But to
Mulch, each cog had a distinctive signature and when a ratchet caught, it was
so loud as to be deafening.

'One,' he breathed.

'Hurry it up, convict. Your time is running out.'

35 'You interrupted to tell me that? I can see now how you made commander,
Julius.'

'Convict, I'm going to …'

But it was no use. Mulch had removed his earpiece, slipping it into his
pocket. Now he could devote his full attention to the task at hand.

40 'Two.'

There was noise outside. In the hall. Someone was coming. About the size of
an elephant by the sound of it. No doubt this was the man mountain that had
made mincemeat of the Retrieval Squad.

Mulch blinked a bead of sweat from his eye. Concentrate. Concentrate. The
45 cogs clicked by. Millimetre by millimetre. Nothing was catching. The floor
seemed to be hopping gently, though he could be imagining it.

Click, click. Come on. Come on. His fingers were slick with perspiration, the
dial slipping between them. Mulch wiped them on his jerkin.

'Now, baby, come on. Talk to me.'

50 *Click. Thunk.*

'Yes!'

Mulch twisted the handle. Nothing. Still an obstruction. He ran a fingertip
over the metal face. There. A small irregularity. A micro keyhole. Too small for
your average lock pick. Time for a little trick he'd learned in prison. Quickly
55 though, his stomach was bubbling like stew in the oven, and the footsteps
were getting closer.

Selecting a sturdy chin hair, Mulch fed it gently into the tiny hole. When the
tip reappeared, he pulled the root from his chin. The hair immediately stiffened,
retaining the shape of the lock's interior.

60 Mulch held his breath and twisted. Smooth as a goblin's lie, the lock opened.
Beautiful. At moments like these, it was almost worth all the jail time.

The kleptomaniac dwarf swung back the little door. Beautiful work. Almost
worthy of a fairy forge. Light as a wafer. Inside was a small chamber. And in the
chamber was …

65 'Oh, gods above,' breathed Mulch. Then things came to a head rather rapidly.
The shock that Mulch had experienced communicated itself to his bowels, and
they decided the excess air had got to go. Mulch knew the symptoms. Jelly
legs, bubbling cramps, wobbly behind. In the seconds remaining to him, he
snatched the object from the safe and, leaning over, he clasped his knees for
70 support.

The constrained wind had built up to mini-cyclone intensity and could not be
constrained. And so it exited.
Rather abrasively. Blowing open Mulch's bum-flap and slamming into the rather
large gentleman who had been sneaking up behind him.

3 Mulch has to deal with three 'tumblers'. What does the writer do to create a suspenseful gap between tumblers 1 and 2, and then between tumblers 2 and 3?

4 How does the introduction of a noise from outside add to the suspense?

5 The writer does not say what is in the safe. Why not?

6 For several lines, the writer has not mentioned whatever has been outside the room. Why not?

7 How does the writer 'release' the tension that has been building up?

Activity 16

Write a short paragraph explaining two techniques the writer has used to create suspense. Use the following starters to help you.

> Two of the techniques used by the writer to create suspense are . . .
>
> You can see the first one in the part where . . .
>
> This creates suspense because . . .
>
> The second technique can be seen in the part where . . .
>
> This creates suspense because . . .

Using short sentences for suspense

Writers deliberately use sentences of different lengths. They often use short sentences to create suspense. Using short sentences breaks a description into smaller units, so the details are built up bit by bit. This can create real suspense for readers.

Activity 17

1 Explore the effects of short sentences by reading these two texts aloud slowly. The first one is from *Artemis Fowl*. The second one has been adapted to make the sentences longer. Why do you think the writer decided to use so many short sentences?

Original text

There was noise outside. In the hall. Someone was coming. About the size of an elephant by the sound of it. No doubt this was the man mountain that had made mincemeat of the Retrieval Squad.

    Mulch blinked a bead of sweat from his eye. Concentrate. Concentrate. The cogs clicked by. Millimetre by millimetre. Nothing was catching. The floor seemed to be hopping gently, though he could be imagining it. (page 165, lines 41–6)

Adapted text

There was a noise outside in the hall. It sounded as if someone about the size of an elephant was coming. No doubt this was the man mountain that had made mincemeat of the Retrieval Squad.

    Mulch blinked a bead of sweat from his eye and told himself to concentrate. The cogs clicked by millimetre by millimetre but nothing was catching. The floor seemed to be hopping gently, though he could be imagining it.

2 Imagine another scene that could be full of suspense. For example, someone is hiding in a room and can hear sounds getting louder outside. The door suddenly opens…

Write a short paragraph describing this situation, finishing as the door opens. Concentrate on using short sentences to build up suspense.

Feedback

1 When you have finished your piece of writing, swap it with a partner. Read your partner's writing and answer the following questions.
  a Has your partner used short sentences?
  b Do the short sentences add detail a little at a time, building up suspense?
  c Are there places where longer sentences could be broken down into shorter ones?

2 Think about your partner's feedback on your writing. Make improvements to your paragraph if you can.

Releasing the tension: anti-climax

When using suspense, a writer builds to a climax when an awaited event happens. After the event the writer lets the tension fall away, creating an anti-climax. In the text on page 165, the writer releases the tension in a comic way.

Activity 18

1 Re-read the short piece of writing you have just completed. It ends with the door suddenly opening.

2 Add two or three sentences that release the tension you have created. What might happen as the door opens that is 'comic' or 'ordinary'? You have built up the suspense, so the reader is expecting something important to happen. But you are going to 'trick' the reader with a surprise ending. This means you will contrast the tension of the opening with the comedy of the ending.

3 Swap your piece with a partner. Say which three things you think work best, and why. Suggest one possible improvement.

Influencing what readers think of characters

When writers create characters, they also shape how readers will respond to them. Some characters are seen as comic, some as attractive, some as loathsome. You are going to explore how the writer of *Artemis Fowl* shapes the way you respond to one character – a troll.

Shaping reader responses

> The story so far...
>
> Mulch, the earth-eating criminal dwarf, rescues 'the Book' of fairy secrets from the safe and takes the opportunity to escape before he can be put back in prison. Meanwhile, Holly has managed to complete 'the ritual' to top up her fairy magic, and is free from the room she was held in but can't yet leave the house. Some of the fairies decide that something must be done even if it puts Holly at risk, so they send in a troll. The troll will kill anything in its way, be it Butler the bodyguard or Holly the fairy. As Butler sees the troll break through the front door in clouds of dust, he protects himself with an old-fashioned suit of armour and prepares to fight.

The troll

Something moved in the dust haze. It was immediately obvious to Butler that the *something* wasn't human. The manservant had been on too many safaris not to recognise an animal when he saw it. He studied the creature's gait. Possibly simian. Similar upper-body structures to an
5 ape, but bigger than any primate Butler had ever seen. If it was an ape, then his handgun wasn't going to be of much use. You could put five rounds in the skull of a bull ape and he'd still have time to eat you before his brain realised he was dead.

But it wasn't an ape. Apes didn't have night eyes. This
10 creature did. Glowing crimson pupils, half-hidden behind shaggy forelocks. Tusks too, but not elephantine. These were curved, with serrated edges. Gutting weapons. Butler felt a tingle low in his stomach. He'd had the feeling once before. On his first day at the Swiss academy. It was fear.

1 From whose point of view is the story told in lines 1–14?

2 What physical features of the troll are focused on?

3 From those physical features, what impression of the troll is given in the second paragraph?

15 The creature stepped clear of the dust haze. Butler gasped. Again, his first since the academy. This was like no adversary he'd ever faced before. The manservant realised instantly what the fairies had done. They had sent in a primal hunter. A creature with no interest in magic or rules. A thing that would simply
20 kill anything in its way, regardless of species. This was the perfect

predator. That much was clear from the meat-ripping points on its teeth, from the dried gore crusted beneath its claws and form the distilled hatred spilling from its eyes.

> 4 Synonyms are words that are alike in meaning. Organise these nouns from lines 15–23 into two pairs of synonyms:
>   - hunter   - thing   - creature   - predator.
>
> 5 By using synonyms, the writer repeats certain descriptive details about the troll and emphasises them. What impression of the troll does the reader get from these nouns?

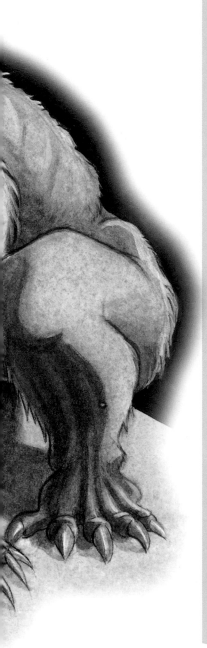

25 The troll shambled forwards, squinting through the chandelier light. Yellowed claws scraped along the marble tiling, throwing up sparks in their wake. It was sniffing now, snorting curious breaths, head cocked to one side. Butler had seen that pose before – on the snouts of starved pit bulls, just before their Russian handlers set them loose on a bear hunt.

> 6 As the troll moves, the writer carefully uses verbs to add to the impression we already have. Which verbs in lines 24–6 emphasise the idea of a slow, ugly, threatening creature?

30 The shaggy head froze, its snout pointed directly at Butler's hiding place. It was no coincidence. The, manservant peeked out between the chain-mail fingers of a gauntlet. Now came the stalk. Once a scent had been acquired, the predator would attempt a slow silent approach, before the lightning strike.

But apparently the troll had not read the predator's handbook, because it didn't bother with the stealth approach, jumping directly to the lightning strike. 35 Moving faster than Butler would have believed possible, the troll sprang across the lobby, brushing the medieval armour aside as though it were a shop mannequin.

> 7 At this stage of the story, whose side is the reader invited to be on? Give reasons for your answer.

The troll fights with Butler and nearly kills him. Holly tries to help, but the troll nearly kills her. As she lies dazed on the floor next to Butler, she touches him 40 *with her magic and heals him, making him stronger than he was before. So pulling his armour back on, he takes on the troll. Butler finds a way past the troll's defences and wounds him badly, while Holly watches . . .*

The troll was concussed, blinded by blood, and lame. A normal person would feel a shard of remorse, but not Butler. He'd seen too many men gored by 45 injured animals. Now was the dangerous time. It was no time for mercy, it was time to terminate with extreme prejudice.

Holly could only watch helplessly as the human took careful aim and delivered a series of crippling blows to the stricken creature. First he took out the tendons, bringing the troll to its knees, then he abandoned the mace and went to work
50 with gauntleted hands, perhaps deadlier than the mace had been. The unfortunate troll fought back pathetically, even managing to land a few glancing blows. But they failed to penetrate the antique armour. Meanwhile Butler toiled like a surgeon. Working on the assumption that the troll and human physiques were basically the same, he rained blow after blow on the dumb creature,
55 reducing it to a heap of quivering fur in so many seconds. It was pitiful to watch. And the manservant wasn't finished yet. He stripped off the bloodied gauntlets, loading a fresh clip into the handgun.

8 The attack on the troll is witnessed by Holly who watches the action 'helplessly'. From the description of Butler's attack, who do you think Holly would help if she could?

9 Why has the writer moved the point of view from Butler to Holly? Suggest two or three possible reasons. Then decide which one you think is the best explanation. Write it down.

Activity 19

1 At the start of the text on page 168, Butler was the prey, or potential victim, and the troll was the vicious hunter. At the end, this has changed. Re-read the final paragraph, lines 47–57. Then copy and complete the table below.

Butler: details from the extract	The impression given
• the human took <u>careful</u> aim and delivered a series of <u>crippling</u> blows	
• he <u>took out</u> the tendons	This suggests he is working like a cold-blooded butcher on this living creature.
• toiled <u>like a surgeon</u>	
• he rained <u>blow after blow</u> on the dumb creature	
The troll: details from the extract	**The impression given**
• the stricken creature	
• The unfortunate troll fought back pathetically	
• The dumb creature	
• It was pitiful to watch	

2 What has the writer done to change the way you react to the troll and to Butler? Use the notes from the tables to help you write a few sentences in response to this question. Use the PEE framework. You could start like this.

POINT   *To change the way the reader responds to the troll, the writer has ...*

EXAMPLE   *You can see this when ...*

EXPLANATION   *This shows ...*

 **Progress check**

1 List three things you have learnt about the techniques writers use to influence the way readers respond to characters.

2 Are there some techniques you have found difficult to understand? Look back through this unit and list the things you need to return to.

Introduction and development of themes

In addition to using language and narrative techniques to tell a story, writers also 'use' stories to explore themes. A 'theme' is an idea explored by a writer – an idea about which the writer often has a very clear point of view.

Artemis Fowl is an action-packed story full of larger-than-life characters, suspense and humour, but it also explores some issues that matter at a deeper level.

The texts that follow are taken from different parts of *Artemis Fowl*. The writer is exploring how humans are ruining the planet and other human weaknesses. He does this by allowing different characters to express opinions about human faults.

Activity 20
Read the five texts on page 172–3. As you read each one, jot down some notes about the idea being explored by the writer. The first one has been done for you.

1

Although she was enjoying the night air, Holly could taste traces of pollutants. The Mud People destroyed everything they came into contact with. Of course they didn't live in the mud any more. Not in this country, at least. Oh no. Big fancy
5 dwellings with rooms for everything – rooms for sleeping, rooms for eating, even a room to go to the toilet! Indoors! Holly shuddered. Imagine going to the toilet inside your own house. Disgusting! The only good thing about going to the toilet was the minerals being returned to the earth, but the Mud People
10 had even managed to botch that up by treating the … stuff … with bottles of blue chemicals. If anyone had told her a hundred years ago that humans would be taking the fertile out of fertiliser, she would have told them to get some air holes drilled in their skull.

In this extract the writer explores how human beings are polluting the planet. The writer is being serious. You can tell this from 'traces of pollutants'. But he also makes a humorous point about indoor toilets. He says they stop humans from fertilising the ground with their waste products.

2

Root tilted his polymer wings, hugging the underside of a fogbank. There was no need to be careful. With his shield activated, he was invisible to the human eye. Even on stealth-sensitive radar he would be no more than a barely perceptible distortion. The commander swooped low to the gunwales.
5 It was an ugly craft, this one. The smell of death and pain lingered in the blood-swabbed decks. Many noble creatures had died here, died and been dissected for a few bars of soap and some heating oil. Root shook his head. Humans were such barbarians.

3

The commander nodded. This was their first break. Fairies had not operated in natural light for centuries. Even when they had lived above ground, they were essentially night creatures. The sun had diluted their magic like bleaching a photograph. If they had to wait another day before sending in a
5 strike force, who knew what damage Fowl could achieve?

It was even possible that this whole affair was media-oriented, and by tomorrow evening Captain Short's face would be on the cover of every publication on the planet. Root shuddered. That would spell the end of everything, unless the Mud People had learned to coexist with other species.
10 And if history had taught him any lessons it was that humans couldn't get along with anyone, even themselves.

4

Mulch would live above ground for a spell. Masquerade as a human dwarf, with an aversion to light. Perhaps buy a penthouse with thick blinds. In Manhattan perhaps, or Monte Carlo. It might seem odd, of course, a dwarf shutting himself away from the sun. But then again, he would be an
5 obscenely rich dwarf. And humans will accept any story, however outlandish, when there's something in it for them. Preferably something green that folds.

5

'The big clue, of course, was Santa Claus.'

Butler's eyebrows nearly jumped off the front of his face.

'Santa Claus?'

Artemis raised his palms. 'I know, I know. I was a tad sceptical myself. But
5   apparently our little corporate-image Santa Claus is not descended from a
Turkish saint, he is a shadow of San D'Klass, the third king of the Frond Elfin
dynasty. He is know as San the Deluded.'

'Not a great title, as titles go.'

'Admittedly. D'Klass thought that the greed of the Mud People in his
10 kingdom could be assuaged by distributing lavish gifts. He would marshal all
the great wizards once a year and have them throw up a great time-stop over
vast regions. Flocks of sprites would be sent out to deliver the presents while
the humans were asleep. Of course, it didn't work. Human greed can never
be assuaged, especially not by gifts.'

 Activity 21

Try writing about a theme of your choice. These guidelines will help you.

1 Invent a character.

2 Think of an outside setting – somewhere to place your character.

3 Your character is waiting for someone or something. Decide what.

4 Write a few sentences from the point of view of the character, about who or what they are waiting for.

5 Write a few sentences about what they notice around them.

6 Gradually introduce a thought into the character's head about the environment and what is being done to it.

For example, you might write about a boy waiting for his mum to pick him up after a football match. He looks around. The area is run-down and there is a lot of litter on the playing field. It makes him think of how wasteful and messy people are.

The end?
After Butler's defeat of the troll, Commander Root decides to take desperate measures to retrieve the fairy gold. He plans to obliterate the inhabitants of Fowl mansion with a biobomb. But does Artemis Fowl have one final ace to play?

To find out, grab a copy of Artemis Fowl and read the exiting conclusion!

Assessment task

MULCH AND THE DOGS

The two texts in this task are from the sequel to *Artemis Fowl*, called *Artemis Fowl: The Arctic Incident*. The questions will help you to focus on how the writer has used language for effect. The piece of writing that you will be asked to produce will also help you to show what you have learnt in this unit. To be successful in this assessment task, you should show a clear understanding of how to use:

- similes
- interesting verbs and adjectives
- short sentences
- other techniques to create comic tone and suspense.

In the text opposite, the writer sets the scene. He also focuses on two different characters – Mulch and the dogs.

The story so far ...
Mulch (the clay-devouring, tunnelling dwarf) is in Los Angeles, where he has been stealing Oscars from film stars. He has been caught in the apartment of Maggie V, trying to steal her Oscar.

Mulch hadn't eaten clay in months, but he still had a few bubbles of gas at his disposal when he needed them.

The dogs were poised to attack. Slobber hung in ribbons from their gaping jaws. He would be torn to pieces. Mulch concentrated. The familiar bubbling
5   began to fill his stomach, pulling it out of shape. It felt as though a couple of gnome garbage wrestlers were going a few rounds in there. The dwarf gritted his teeth, this was going to be a big one.

The handler blew a football whistle. The dogs lunged forward like torpedoes with teeth. Mulch let go with a stream of gas, blowing a hole in the rug and
10   propelling himself to the ceiling, where his thirsty pores anchored him. Safe. For the moment.

The German Shepherds were particularly surprised. In their time they had chewed their way through most creatures in the food chain. This was something new. And not altogether pleasant. You have to remember that a
15   dog's nose is far more sensitive than a human one.

---

1   How does the writer use language to make the dogs seem dangerous? Find one simile, one verb and one adjective that he uses to describe the dogs. Explain the effect these words have on the reader.

2   When describing Mulch's situation, the writer uses two very short sentences:

'Safe. For the moment.' (lines 10–11)

He could easily have written them as one sentence: 'Safe for the moment.' Why do you think he chose to write them as two sentences?

Now read on.

The handler blew his whistle a few more times, but any control he might have had disappeared the moment Mulch flew through the air on a jet of recycled wind. As soon as the dogs' nasal passages cleared, they began to leap, teeth gnashing at the apex.
20   Mulch swallowed. Dogs are smarter than the average goblin. It was only a matter of time before they thought to scale the furniture and make a jump from there.

Mulch made for the window, but the handler was there before him, blocking the hole with his padded body. Mulch noticed him fumbling with a weapon at
25   his belt. This was getting serious. Dwarfs are many things, but bulletproof is not one of them.

To make matters worse, Maggie V appeared at the bedroom door, brandishing a chrome baseball bat. This was not the Maggie V the public was used to. Her face was covered with a green mask, and there appeared to be a
30   tea bag taped under each eye.

3 Write a continuation of this scene (about 200 words) using some of the techniques you have developed in this unit. Follow the steps below to help you.

Step 1

Think about what might happen next.

- Will Mulch escape or remain trapped?
- How could Mulch avoid being eaten by the dogs or hit by Maggie V? He is a dwarf who can munch his way through things and expel gases at extreme pressure. Dwarves also have the power to speak dog language.

Step 2

When you have some ideas about WHAT will happen next, think about HOW you will write it. What techniques will you use? Remind yourself of the techniques covered in this unit:

- using effective similes, verbs, adverbs and adjectives
- combining dialogue and interesting narrative detail
- writing in a comic tone by using such techniques as exaggerated alliteration, onomatopoeia and comic similes
- using short sentences to build up suspense.

Step 3

Spend some time thinking about WHERE you will use these techniques.

- If you use dialogue, you will have to think about who talks to whom – Maggie V to Mulch is the most obvious possibility.
- If you use dialogue you should also add interesting narrative detail (see pages 157–8).
- If you are focusing on a character, remember that you can create characteristics through thoughts, behaviour, dialogue and descriptive detail. You may decide to introduce a new character of your own.

Step 4

Write a first draft of your continuation concentrating on WHAT happens.

Step 5

When you have finished your first draft, read through it again carefully. Look at the list of techniques above to check you have used them all. Make changes to your first draft to introduce any missing or ineffective techniques.

Step 6

Finally, when you are satisfied with your work, write out a final version.